GHOSTS OF
Coeur d'Alene
AND THE
Silver Valley

DEBORAH CUYLE

HAUNTED
America

Published by Haunted America
A Division of The History Press
Charleston, SC
www.historypress.com

Cover: The Roosevelt Inn in Coeur d'Alene is haunted by two ghosts: a little boy and a previous teacher from its schoolhouse days. *Courtesy of author.*

First published 2020

ISBN 9781540243867

Library of Congress Control Number: 2020932080

I dedicate this book to my incredible son, Dane Brown, who has always been my best friend and cohort in a passion for writing. Also, to my wonderful Middy, who never complains when I am writing nonstop even though a yummy dinner and couple cold cocktails are waiting for me to share with him. My appreciation also goes to all my spiritual BFFs, who have joined me in a little ghost hunting and support my paranormal research and beliefs. An open mind is an open door. I personally have experienced so many things I cannot explain that I can no longer even remotely doubt the existence of ghosts or spirits. In fact, the one hundred-plus-year-old home I am living in now, in the quaint old silver mining town of Wallace in the Coeur d'Alene region, is extremely haunted by two friendly ghosts!

And last but not least, to my incredible and loving mom, Roxine, who always believed I could do whatever I set my mind to do. I swear she somehow still visits my sisters and me in times of sorrow or if we are just missing her.

My books are also dedicated to all of my fellow ghost hunters out there. Without them, I would be wandering around dark rooms all by myself with my EMF detector and my cell phone application Ghost Radar…and that wouldn't be very much fun at all.

Happy ghost hunting!
Deb

CONTENTS

CONTENTS

PREFACE

I hope readers visit many of these sites as they learn about the fascinating history of each of these haunted places. As is common with my books, I try to incorporate as many historical facts, names and dates as possible in each chapter. I feel this brings the ghosts and their stories to life and makes learning about the towns more interesting. Many of my readers tell me they enjoy both—learning about the town's history *while* reading about the local spirits that haunt them. I love hearing a good ghost story, and after researching the building, I can actually find evidence of someone with that name who really lived at that location (or died there) at one time or another.

Being an NDE (near death experience) survivor, I am probably a little more open-minded than most people. Perhaps someday science can prove what really happens to us after we die—the eternal mystery questioned by every living being—but until the riddle is solved, it is all just speculation. Religion and science may someday agree, but they likely will not. I see both sides of the debate. Too many unexplained events happen to each of us to not entertain the idea of ghosts and the spirit world. I read somewhere that God or spirits do give us signs when we ask for them, but we, as humans, are too busy or too close-minded to see them or recognize them. I often wonder what life would be like if people were not so skeptical of the possibility of the spirit world. How would that change the way people behave on earth today? Would it be reassuring or terrifying to most people? I am often baffled by people who tell me that they believe in the afterlife but not in spirits. How can the two really be separated? Perhaps some dead people just choose to haunt a place while other spirits choose not to? It is a wonderful mystery.

This recent book project exists because I'm currently living in the Coeur d'Alene region and falling in love with it. I have great interest and respect for the early pioneers and a fascination for local history and old buildings. I love all the lore and legends about ghosts and spirits that people have told me. It is fun to walk the same streets today that early settlers once walked and think of how it was back in the old days. When I look at old brick buildings or original hardwood floors, I try to imagine the thousands of people who once walked these streets or visited these buildings, the horses that pulled wagons and goods, the gunslingers and outlaws, the bartenders and shopkeepers—all of them living their lives and going about their business, just as we do today. I would have loved to have been alive in the late 1800s. I just saw a huge safe from the late 1800s that has a bullet indentation in its side from an old murder that occurred here in Wallace.

History is full of people who haunt us, who want to be recognized and never forgotten for what they accomplished while alive—the improvements they created for a town or what they offered their family and community. This book is about those fascinating spirits—the spirited people who made beautiful Coeur d'Alene and the Silver Valley what it is today.

Most of the stories were told to me by locals and some have been pulled out of old newspapers—all told out of fun for the love of history and lore. The book is *not* intended to be a nonfiction project, and even after hundreds of hours hunched over reading and researching, I still found conflicting dates and inconsistent historic details, so please take it for what it is. I tried to be as accurate with names, dates and details as possible, but this is mostly a book full of tales of many mischievous ghosts and the interesting history of Coeur d'Alene and the nearby towns nestled in the Silver Valley. Enjoy!

ACKNOWLEDGEMENTS

Behind every man now alive stands 30 ghosts,
for that is the ratio by which the dead outnumber the living.
—*Arthur C. Clarke,* 2001: A Space Odyssey

There are many people to thank for this endeavor, and without their help and guidance, this book would not have been possible. My wonderful editor, Artie Crisp, has been such a pleasure to work with, along with all of the other incredible people at Arcadia Publishing and The History Press. Their mission to promote local history is passionate and infectious, and I am blessed to work on my books with them. Their dedication to recording local history is nothing less than amazing, and without them, many books would never be written.

My appreciation is extended to all those who took the time to share their personal ghost stories and experiences—without them this book would not have the extra flair that I love so much.

And as always, I want to thank every single person who does what they can to preserve history—whether it is volunteering at the local historical society, maintaining old cemeteries and gravestones that would otherwise be neglected or simply researching their private genealogy through sites like ancestry.com. In this fast-paced and high-tech world, the past can unfortunately be forgotten and every effort to maintain and record valuable data, photographs, diaries, documents and records is of the utmost importance for future generations.

ACKNOWLEDGEMENTS

One final request, *please do not disturb or trespass on any of the locations listed throughout this book without permission from the property or business owners*, as some have experienced property destruction, and this is unfortunate. Thank you for understanding.

INTRODUCTION

"Do you really want to know where we come from?" she said. "In every century, in every country, they'll call us something different. They'll say we're ghosts, angels, demons, elemental spirits, and giving us a name doesn't help anybody. When did a name change what someone is?"
—Brenna Yovanoff

Coeur d'Alene—even the sound of the name rolls off the tongue in a magical and beautiful way, which fits the city perfectly. For the region of northern Idaho, not many places can compete in beauty, cleanliness, friendliness, great food, art and music—all of the things people love. And to make it even more inviting, surrounding the city is gorgeous, deep blue water and picturesque mountains. It is no wonder that by 1909, Coeur d'Alene had earned the namesake of the "City of Beautiful Homes" because many people were moving there for its ideal climate and breathtaking scenery. The population quickly grew to over nine thousand residents. Its splendor drew some of the wealthiest people in the United States to its 135 miles of lake shores, and it soon earned another nickname from the elites, the "Scenic City by an Unsalted Sea."

Yet the actual name "Coeur d'Alene" originated with the French fur traders and trappers, as they considered the native tribespeople to have extremely sharp minds when it came to conducting business. The translation is "Heart of Awl." (An awl is a sharp leather punch tool.) In the 1800s, fur traders and explorers were drawn to the lakeside area of Coeur d'Alene not just because

Early Coeur d'Alene from Tubbs Hill, circa 1915. As early as 1909, the waterfront was filled in to accommodate industry and transportation. The diagonal boardwalk (*center foreground*) was built by the Red Collar Line to connect passengers on the Electric Line Railroad at Independence Point with the Northern Pacific Line at the Third Street dock. The Milwaukee depot is center near the waterfront and the new fill. The Northern Pacific depot is on the right. *Courtesy of the Museum of Northern Idaho CDA-9-13.*

it was so beautiful and inviting but also because its waters were plentiful with fish and the soil was fertile for growing. In 1883, a few permanent buildings finally popped up: a general store, a brewery, the Coeur d'Alene Inn, the Fashion Saloon, Fatty Carrol's Dance Hall and the Hotel d'Landing. That same year, Coeur d'Alene somehow became home to over twenty saloons—more than its share of bars needed to entertain locals and tourists. One of the earliest known settlers of the area was a man name McAndrews, who always carried a revolver. When McAndrews began drinking and swinging his gun around, most people headed to the safety of their homes. One day though, mouthy McAndrews was not so lucky, and another man shot him and ended his life right then and there.

Founded in 1887, the small town consisted of just a mere forty residents. (Now, Coeur d'Alene is home to almost fifty-four thousand lucky people.) The first of several positions in town were quickly developed: postmaster was V.W. Sander, drugstore owner was Jack Couvaland, blacksmith was James Tracy and the first carpenter was Sam Smith. It is documented that during the first year of excavations for the small town, many skeletons were found while digging. Where did these skeletons come from? Who were the people buried? Many unanswered questions still exist. Many tales and legends surround local stories, but clues and evidence rarely exist. Any of these unclaimed bodies could be some of the spirits that still roam the streets of Coeur d'Alene today.

Old newspapers echo tales of desperate gamblers and prospectors who risked everything in search of nearby treasures found deep in the mountains of the Silver Valley. Today, if the walls could talk in the buildings that still stand in small towns that make up the Silver Valley, they would whisper dark tales of hushed murders, devastating fires and unfortunate mining disasters. North Idaho College was once part of Fort Sherman, and full body apparitions of a man in war-type attire walks the halls and grounds. At the four-thousand-acre Farragut State Park (a former World War II naval training center), it is rumored that a German prisoner of war throws rocks and pushes visitors. In a real place called Bates Motel (once used for barracks for officers of war), rooms 1 and 3 are reportedly haunted.

The long stretch called the Silver Valley has many ghostly places among the small towns. In Kellogg, a grumpy saloon owner killed a man in 1906, and his victim reportedly still seeks revenge. In the same town in the year 1972, ninety-one men lost their lives in the devastating Sunshine Mine disaster. In Cataldo, some claim the spirit of a young girl named Abigail lingers by her grave in a nearby cemetery. The historic mining town of Wallace is the home to many ghosts. "Maggie" in the Jameson Hotel fusses about the rooms, the spirit of Miss Montgomery roams the halls in the Ryan Hotel, and it is possible that the ghost of an old barkeep dislikes the way the current bartender at a local pub mixes his drinks. There are many tales of skulls falling from chimneys, dusty ledgers with century-old secrets, expensive gems hidden behind walls in mansions, silver and golds bars being found in rafters during remodels and much more.

These and many other ghosts want their stories told as their restless spirits linger—twitchy for revenge and hopeful for acknowledgment or still searching for their long-anticipated mother lode of silver and gold.

Follow these stories from Coeur d'Alene all the way east through the Silver Valley region, where many ghosts still linger more than a century after they left this world.

PART I.

COEUR D'ALENE HAUNTS

The thing I find really scary about ghosts and demons is that you don't really know what they are or where they are. They're not very well understood. You don't know what they want from you. So it's the kind of thing you don't even know how to defend yourself against. Anything that's unknown and mysterious is very scary.

—*Oren Peli*

1

COEUR D'ALENE

A Beautiful Yet Very Haunted City

Ghosts—a single word that conjures up all sorts of images and ideas about the spirit world. Hauntings and ghostly spirits have been around as long as humans and evoke every emotion from fear to intrigue to refusal of belief. Every culture treats death and the spirit world differently—different rituals, customs, burial practices—but all have one thing in common: the afterlife.

Ghost stories, legends and folklore exist in any town—big or small, new or old—as human beings are fascinated with the afterlife and are eager to capture "proof" of the spirit world. Apparitions are the most common form of paranormal activity. An animal or a person who keeps reappearing at a location over and over again is classified as an actual "haunting." An important characteristic of a classic haunting is noises. These noises imitate the sounds of human and animal activities, such as crying, chairs moving, dishes breaking or dogs barking.

Another form of activity is called the "crisis apparition." These are single events that typically occur when a living person undergoes a crisis and a loved one appears to offer them comfort. These crisis apparitions are commonly shrugged off as daydreams or ignored and labeled as strange flukes caused by stress. With all the tragedies local citizens suffered, crisis apparitions would seem most likely.

So, Coeur d'Alene has its fair share of ghosts, indeed.

ROOSEVELT INN

Where Two Ghosts Thrive

A ghost story from John Hough, current owner of the Roosevelt Inn:

Our ghost is a friendly 7-year-old boy that we have named Dennis. When a paranormal investigator asked the spirit if he liked to be called "Dennis," the response was "yes." Dennis is our most active and friendly ghost. When we leave town, he throws a little tantrum. One time he unscrewed all the lightbulbs in the third-floor ceiling. I thought maybe a fuse was blown, but they all checked out. There are thirty-eight bulbs on the third floor, and it takes a ladder to get to them. Even the lights inside the ceiling fan were unscrewed! Dennis is notorious for waving at guests. He appears to always be happy, although he can be a bit mischievous. In 2008, the Roosevelt underwent a major remodel in the attic and lower level. My worker Mark always had a three-gallon thermos of Gatorade or water, since it was June and very hot. One time, Mark could not find his water. We were hanging sheetrock, and it was pretty dusty. Mark thought I was messing with him, but I was not. I did not move his water. There was no sheetrock dust where his water had been. We decided to take a lunch break and go downstairs to make peanut butter and jelly sandwiches. Mark was a little bothered by not finding his water jug. When we went back upstairs to work, his water jug was back. Mark said, "Dude, you could have told me you had a ghost!"

Another time, our daughter was in the kitchen and all the magnets came flying off the fridge. The pictures and papers they were holding up started to stick to my daughter. My daughter just yelled, "Dennis, quit it!"

My wife was in the kitchen making cookies, and all the cabinet doors kept opening and closing by themselves. She would close the cabinet doors and they would reopen. My wife asked, "Dennis, do you enjoy the spices?"

Another ghost we have is a female apparition, who appears to be in her mid-fifties. She wears a white dress, her hair is pulled back and in a bun cap, the dress has buttons all the way up to her neck collar and long sleeves. She never has any feet; it is like she is floating. She was not happy about the renovations. We believe it is the spirit of a teacher named Ms. Millenious that worked at the school in the '40s and '50s. She committed suicide in one of the little cottages that were across the street for the teachers to live in. In those days, female teachers were not allowed to get married. Possibly she

The Roosevelt schoolhouse on a postcard around 1910. It's one of the most prominent haunted buildings in Coeur d'Alene. *Courtesy of Wikipedia public domain.*

killed herself because she never had the chance to have a family life herself, and then she became too old to have one. We have photographs of her in the halls with the children from her classes.

The Roosevelt has a long history in Coeur d'Alene. Constructed in 1905 as a school for the first through sixth grades, the Roosevelt School taught all of the local children. In 1906, the four teachers were Miss Leischn, Miss Emerson, Ida Marsh and Miss Rauch. As the Coeur d'Alene population grew in the 1940s, the school no longer taught the fifth and sixth graders. The Roosevelt continued operating as a school until 1971, when a larger and more modern school was built. From 1971 through 1979, the board of education used the Roosevelt for storage. In 1979, it was sold to Jonas Marias, who converted the school into office spaces and added the third floor. He also changed the ceiling heights from eighteen feet to ten feet, and the offices were rented until 1992, when it was converted again to a bed-and-breakfast. John and Tina Hough purchased the building in 1999 and still run and operate the inn. The ambitious Hough's tore out walls and opened up the rooms, added the beautiful archways, removed several doors to make the rooms more spacious, created the gorgeous landscaping and fountain, installed the fence, planted the grass and trees and much

The Roosevelt Inn is haunted by Miss Millenious, a teacher who committed suicide in a cottage across the street. *Courtesy of John and Tina Hough, Roosevelt Inn.*

more. Interestingly, John Hough attended the Roosevelt School as a student from first to fourth grade, and his childhood photographs can be found in the hanging in the halls. Is Coeur d'Alene's famous century-old Roosevelt Inn actually haunted? If you ask the owners and their employees, you will get a firm yes!

FATTY CARROLL

A Man to Never Cross

Coeur d'Alene was a hard town in the early days. It was considered one of the roughest towns between Portland and Saint Paul. Wyatt Earp even tried to tame it when he became its sheriff in 1884. One of the most feared men of those days was Jim Metzger, also known as Fatty Carroll. Fatty owned seventy acres on the river and everyone knew not to cross him—or you wouldn't live to tell about it. His place was called the Variety Saloon in 1887, and in 1897, it became a gaming resort called Bonanza City, where faro cards and plenty of gambling ensued. Fatty's business flourished in the 1880s, and his place was considered one of the toughest in the country. No one crossed Fatty. If they did, they might end up in a shallow grave in his private cemetery. Some say that Fatty had a house that was built over the Spokane River, and if he invited you to his place, you needed to steer clear of his trap door in the floor, or you might wind up in the bottom of the river.

There were rumors of a very wealthy man who visited Coeur d'Alene, and he was never heard from again nor was his body ever found. Did he fall victim to Fatty?

Fatty also owned a brothel on the corner of Fourth and Sherman in Coeur d'Alene. Later, when workers were prepping the ground for a foundation for the new Wilson's Pharmacy, several skeletons were found in shallow graves. These were believed to be the three missing Indians and five missing soldiers from Fort Sherman in 1887. Did these unfortunate men somehow anger Fatty, thus coming to their demise? That same year, one of Fatty's buildings caught fire, and two men lost their lives; Lottie Haines, who was sleeping, burned to death, and "Uncle John" died while trying to retrieve his personal belongings from the building.

In the early 1900s, more skeletons were found near Tubbs Hill, where Carroll's Variety once was. When the Coeur d'Alene & Spokane Railway Company was excavating the car barn, workers found multiple skeletons buried beneath a few feet of soil. These were thought to be the remains of the missing soldiers, since it was very near Fort Sherman at that time. In the years 1901 through 1903, four sets of bodies were discovered. The first were at the Coeur d'Alene Lumber Company—the old site of Fatty Carrols ranch and gambling center. Fatty had sold his property to the lumber company for the development of a sawmill in 1902. The second set was found at what was termed Dr. Scallon's Block, located on the corner of Fourth and Sherman, which is where Fatty owned the brothel that later became the Wilson's Drugstore. In 1903, the third set of bodies was discovered between Mullan Road and Fort Sherman. Interestingly, even in 2018, construction workers unearthed more human remains at the block of Mullan Avenue. Who do those bones belong to?

Did all these unfortunate victims die at the hand of the terrible Fatty Carroll? Do any of these victims haunt the sites where their remains are found? With no concrete evidence of who the victims are, it is hard to say or research.

Fatty was no stranger to crime. In 1897, he went in front of Judge Will for assault and battery against a shoemaker named Bade Grundt, who had his shop in Fatty's building. In 1903, Fatty was charged with disorderly conduct when he tangled with a man named John Garton at the Crystal Saloon located at the corner of Main Avenue and Division Street. Garton kicked

Fatty right in the face while he was down on the ground. There are no records of Fatty ever going to prison for any of these crimes.

And even in 2019, more bones were found near Tubbs Hill, which were never identified, except that they were "very old" in nature. Could these be some of Fatty's victims? The world may never know. But one thing is certain: Fatty Carroll was one man no one ever wanted on their bad side, or they might not live to see the sun rise.

O'REILLY'S SALOON

The Missing Soldiers

Coeur d'Alene was troubled by criminals and murderers—many living and working in plain sight. More skeletons were discovered in 1903 while workers were digging to excavate a forty-foot roadway for the Spokane & Coeur d'Alene electric line. More missing soldiers? Possibly miners? The area being excavated was the site of a former saloon called O'Reilly's, run by Ed O'Reilly, a former soldier himself. During its heyday, soldiers were lured to O'Reilly's on payday to partake in gambling, drinking and the comfort of women. Many never returned to their post the next morning and were presumably "deserters" of the army, thus no follow-up investigations were conducted by the police.

O'Reilly's was originally built in 1886 and featured a saloon out front, a back room where French women would entertain guests and a fenced back lot and stables/harness shop. This back lot is where the bodies were found in 1903. It was believed that the soldiers were murdered in cold blood and their paycheck money stolen. Were the French prostitutes in on the scheme? Sometimes two or three men would go missing in a day. In 1891, the *Kootenai Herald* listed saloon license bonds and the name "O'Reilly & White" appears, so the story holds true that there was a saloon there. The O'Reilly Saloon continued to operate until it burned down in 1893. O'Reilly did not have the best reputation in town, and he was eventually run out of Coeur d'Alene by the locals. Did the murderous spree end after he left town?

Around seven skeletons were found by the excavation crew—none of the bodies were in coffins, and their bodies were obviously quickly buried under approximately two feet of soil. The deceased had no identifying clothing, jewelry or personal items on them that could help identify their bodies. More skeletons were later found in the city limits. Nothing is known about these victims either.

Was there a cold-blooded serial killer on the loose in Coeur d'Alene? Was Fatty Carroll that killer? Do the restless souls of all of the unknown men still roam Coeur d'Alene, seeking revenge or at least recognition?

FORT SHERMAN/NORTH IDAHO COLLEGE

A Haunted School

Many employees and students feel they have experienced paranormal activities in certain areas of North Idaho College. In particular, the area of Boswell Hall and in the auditorium areas. The apparition of a man wearing some type of war outfit or uniform is often seen roaming the halls and grounds. It is noted that he can walk right through the walls. Others report the sounds of heavy footsteps when no one else is in the room or hallway. No one knows exactly who the ghost is, but some have theories. Perhaps it is the ghost of one of the men from the army who was killed. Maybe it is a spirit who is compelled to stay in the building for unknown reasons. Is the area haunted by one of the men killed there? As for now, the identity of the ghost or ghosts remains a mystery.

Yet the buildings and grounds are rich in Idaho history. In 1877, General William T. Sherman (1820–1891) proposed that a military fort be built on the shore of Lake Coeur d'Alene, as he found the area particularly beautiful and a great location because it would be situated right by the river. The main reasons to build a fort there were to protect the locals from the Indians, to protect the telegraph and railroads crews from harm and to guard the Canadian border. The building of the fort soon prompted the gathering of about forty local people who would cater to the soldiers and provide services, food and goods. The construction of several smaller buildings soon occurred and became the start of what is known today as the Coeur d'Alene area. The soldiers would call today's area of City Beach "Sudstown" because the local women would wash the soldier's cloths on the rocks by the water, creating a sudsy mess. As beautiful as it was, the soldiers complained about the location often, as it was prone to extreme flooding that at times made the buildings inhabitable. In 1879, the name was changed from Camp Sherman to Fort Coeur d'Alene.

Around 1887, a sinister side to the fort began to emerge. On payday, soldiers would go into town to enjoy a few drinks, dance and gamble, but some never returned. Their disappearance was shrugged off as men deserting their duties, but a few years later, while workers were building a foundation for the new Wilson's Pharmacy on Fourth and Sherman Avenue, several corpses turned up. Legend says that a ruthless man named "Fatty" Carroll had a habit of disposing of people he didn't get along with or who owed him money. Visitors today claim to still feel the eerie chill of cold spikes and a creepy sensation while in the area where these bodies were found.

Disappearing soldiers and Indians aside, in 1887, the name changed again from Fort Coeur d'Alene to Fort Sherman in honor of General William T. Sherman.

Today, the Fort Sherman Chapel is also Coeur d'Alene's oldest church and the site of the first school in the town. Abandoned in 1900, the vacant buildings soon went to auction. Prior to selling, the government set aside twenty acres for a park and twenty acres for a cemetery. Stack & Gibbs purchased the remaining acres but soon went bankrupt.

General Sherman ordered construction in the late 1870s. Three buildings remain of Fort Sherman, where North Idaho College is now located. *Courtesy of Library of Congress, item no. 2016864825.*

In January 1918, the fort went up for auction—one bid was a mere $2,000 produced by Devan & Company from Spokane. It was appraised for $12,000 at the time. Today, a house on the water can sell for well over one million dollars. The Fort Sherman Cemetery was purchased by the city and is now called Forest Cemetery. The famous actress Patty Duke is buried there. There are sure to be many restless spirits roaming that cemetery.

Today, the fort is part of North Idaho College. Only three of the original fort buildings remain in use: the chapel, the officer's quarters and the powder magazine building. The chapel became part of the Museum of North Idaho in 1984 and has been repaired and preserved for future generations to enjoy. Local historian Robert Singletary dresses in costume and hosts interesting talks, and the museum has tours for the public and its members to enjoy.

FERRAGUT STATE PARK

The Spirits of Prisoners

A ghost story from Mark Porter of Spokane Paranormal Society:

Back in the fall of 2017, I was investigating the exterior of the brig myself since the building was closed for the season. The first instance I had with the paranormal was at a window on the eastern side of the building. I asked the entity inside to tap once for "yes" and two for "no," and after a series of questions on four different occasions, I received a tap after each question. The second experience was on the western side of the building by the fire door, where I heard tapping on the door. My K2 meter was lighting up, and I had a rock thrown at me when I was there. The story goes, when it was a prisoner of war camp toward the end of World War II, a German POW was tortured and gave a little bit of information up. The interrogators decided to interrogate a little harder to get more information. The prisoner died in that building.

A well-known haunt near Coeur d'Alene is Farragut State Park in Athol. The brig building is reportedly haunted. People see full-body apparitions, experience being touched, have objects thrown at them, smell peculiar odors and hear voices when no one else is around. Rumors of a suicide and a murder happened on base, and employees still experience strange happenings at the site years later. It is named after the first admiral in the U.S. Navy, David Glasgow Farragut (1801–1870), who was the leading naval officer during the Civil War period. The facility was built after the bombing of Pearl Harbor. The site was built in less than a year, employing over twenty thousand people and cost more than $100 million to construct.

It was once a World War II U.S. Naval training center, where approximately 300,000 men received training in the two and half years it was open. At one time, it used as a prisoner of war camp, housing almost one thousand Germans who were put to work at the facility. One of these German prisoners was rumored to have been killed, and his remains were never given a proper burial. Could this unfortunate German man be the restless soul who haunts the brig? The ghost is sometimes seen wearing some sort of jail uniform.

The military jail, which held men who did not comply with the rules, is now a museum. The land was transferred to the State of Idaho in 1949

Farragut State Park was once a World War II training center run by Admiral David Farragut. A German prisoner was captured and killed there. *Courtesy of the Library of Congress, item no. LC-BH82-4054.*

and became a state park in 1965. It is also listed on the National Register of Historic Places. Many say they can hear heavy chains clanking at night, as if prisoners are still roaming the grounds.

Now a four-thousand-acre camping site, the area has a large statue of a sailor near the museum. Oddly, the faces of the soldiers carved in the statue can play a trick on the eye, and it appears as if the faces move around and stare back at onlookers.

Many hiking trails are located throughout the park, and guests have seen odd lights, eerie sounds and shadowy figures. Hikers report that the closer to the water one gets, the more paranormal activity that occurs.

SPIRIT LAKE

Real Life Romeo and Juliet

The small town of Spirit Lake was established in 1908, and soon grew to one thousand people. It was often referred to as the "handsomest little town in Northern Idaho." Its main industry was lumber, with the $300,000 mill built by Panhandle Lumber Company eagerly churning out 125,000 feet of cut lumber every ten hours. The first school was built in December 1907, with a proud seven pupils taught by a teacher named Miss Emma House. The town was quickly known for its beautiful nearby lake.

Today, nearly two thousand people live in Spirit Lake, and that number doubles during the summer months. Many enjoy the six and a half miles of hiking and biking trails that follow the water, named the Empire Trails.

But the lake holds more than just beauty and charm for locals and tourists. Legend has it that the spirit of a beautiful Indian girl can be seen slowly drifting in her canoe looking for her lover. The Indians originally named the water Lake Kaniskee, which translates to "Lake of the Spirit." Some say the tribe called the water "Tesemini" or "Clear Water." Either way, the lake is one of two in the world that has a clay-sealed bottom and to this day is one of the most spectacular lakes around.

So, who was this Indian girl? It is said that the local Kootenai tribe promised the chief's daughter to another tribe to make peace between the two groups. Yet the daughter was already in love with a young, handsome warrior in her own tribe. This arrangement did not go over well with the two lovers, and they vowed to take their love into the eternal spirit world. They rowed their canoe into the middle of the lake and committed suicide. There are rumors of the sounds of hauntingly beautiful cries coming from the depths of the deep lake as a fog slowly rises over its glistening water. Could it be the two lovers searching for each other? Is it their parents grieving with sorrow over the loss of their children?

Other legends tell of a prospector who lived alone by the lake in the late 1800s, constantly searching for his fortune. Never finding one, his desire to be rich eventually drove him mad and frustrated. In a fury, he burned his cabin down and then rowed out into the lake and killed himself.

Yet another legend of the lake involves a wolf and an old spirit named Amotkan. Amotkan supposedly ruled the lake, and for some reason, it grew angry at the local people, so it decided to dry up the area, withholding water from the villagers for punishment. A small wolf wandered by in search of

Spirit Lake is haunted by an Indian girl who took her life by drowning. *Courtesy of Library of Congress, photographer Edward S. Curtis.*

water to quench its thirst and, unable to find any, turned on the sleeping spirit Amotkan and killed him. The death of Amotkan released the spell, and soon, water was flowing freely again. Unfortunately, the land began to flood. The body of Amotkan was carried down the river until it ended up in Cataldo near the mission. The heart of Amotkan was torn out and thrown on the land, thus the land was termed "Pointed Heart."

No one will ever really know who (or what) is haunting the crystal blue waters of Spirit Lake.

BATES MOTEL

Haunted Before *Psycho*

The interesting history of the Bates Motel building began before World War II, as the building was used as a barracks for the officers. When the war finally ended, the building was sold and turned into a motel called the

The Bates Motel in Coeur d'Alene was reportedly haunted long before the famous movie *Psycho* or the television series. *Courtesy of Shirley Jess Photography.*

Roadway Inn. A few years later, a local accountant, Randy Bates, bought it and renamed it the Bates Motel. (It was haunted long before the movie *Psycho* was released.) After the movie, the Bates Hotel gained more interest from locals and tourists. Some suggest that the writer of the thriller, Robert Bloch (1917–1994), actually roomed at the hotel sometime in the 1950s, and his inspiration came from his eerie experiences. The Bates Motel in the movie and the Bates Motel in Coeur d'Alene are *not* the same location or building—they just share the same name. No one in the showers of the Bates Motel in Coeur d'Alene gets stabbed to death like in the movie. But visitors probably have disturbing thoughts and images in mind if they have ever seen the movie.

The Bates Motel is located at 2018 Sherman Avenue in Coeur d' Alene, and of its thirteen rooms, numbers 1 and 3 are reportedly haunted. Employees and guests tell of experiencing icy cold sensations, the feeling of being watched when no one else is in the room, lights blinking, odd noises and items moving by themselves. Who or what is haunting the Bates Motel? Is it just active imaginations? Perhaps stay the night and see what you experience.

D-MAC'S ON HAUSER-LAKE

Dine with a Ghost

Known to be haunted, the wonderful restaurant called D-Mac's near Hauser Lake is said to have two spirits who haunt it. The building is situated where an old residence once stood during the late 1800s. Then during World War

II, it became a restaurant and bar. Like many of the old buildings in Idaho, it was said to be a brothel at one point. Since then, it has been called a number of different places, such as the Cliff House Resort, the Club, the Rainbow Inn and Blackjacks Saloon and Grill.

One ghost is said to be that of a beautiful lady who is always seen wearing a white dress. Her name was Maddie. The story goes that Maddie used to work in the brothel, and she somehow ended up dead—possibly even murdered. Maddie played the piano for guests during her tenure. Her spirit now tends to hang out in the bar area. She enjoys the laughter and night life as much now as when she was alive. Employees and guests report unexplainable sounds and voices while dining at D-Mac's. Others claim to be touched by an invisible hand. Paranormal groups have used flashlights to try to communicate with Maddie or any other ghosts who haunt D-Macs, and incredibly, the flashlight does turn on and off during a session of questions. Maddie is said to be a very happy spirit and enjoys hanging out with people at the bar.

PART II.

THE SILVER VALLEY GHOSTS

We tell stories of the dead as a way of making a sense of the living. More than just simple urban legends and campfire tales, ghost stories reveal the contours of our anxieties, the nature of our collective fears and desires, the things we can't talk about in any other way. The past we're most afraid to speak aloud of in the bright light of day is the same past that tends to linger in the ghost stories we whisper in the dark.

—Colin Dickey,
Ghostland: An American History in Haunted Places

I daho boasts several ghost towns, or *almost* ghost towns, all with their own stories to tell anyone eager enough to listen. Sometimes artifacts remain long after the town itself has been destroyed or burned down. Scraps of rusty metal, worn-out timbers, smooth logs of mining core samples, abandoned houses and mines all litter the land of Idaho and are sometimes all that remains of the bustling silver and gold rushes that stormed through the state. Men heard of the promise of riches in Idaho and would travel for hundreds of miles in search of their fortune. Some did indeed strike it rich, while others sadly left empty-handed. During those productive years, there were certain rules when claiming a stake. Men could only stake one claim at a time, the claim had to be clearly marked and it had to be recorded in town. Claims could be as small as a few square feet running up to several hundred square feet in size. Another rule was that the claimant had to actually work the land—if he didn't, the claim could go to someone more eager. True hard-working miners could hardly be troubled by lollygaggers or looky-loos, and there were only a few things that could disturb their interest in striking it rich, including theft, murder or someone jumping their claim, which might result in a murder.

Old barns from years gone by and homes in ghost towns are becoming rarer as land becomes more valuable. *Courtesy of author.*

The era of silver and gold mining is still active in parts, but the silent remains are more common than up-and-running mines. If the echoes of old-timers could bounce off the watery, hard walls inside the mines or the now-abandoned cabins they once lived in, what interesting stories would they tell?

2

CATALDO MISSION

The Prophecy of Circling Raven

Located just twenty-three miles east of Coeur d'Alene, the Sacred Heart Mission building is the oldest standing building in Idaho. Local legend tells that when Father Pierre-Jean DeSmet (1801–1873) met with the Lake Coeur d'Alene tribe, an Indian prophet named Circling Raven came to him and predicted that "light-skinned men in long black robes would come to the people here with a new religion that would change their lives forever." Was Circling Raven's vision an actual prophecy or just a good hunch? Either way, the prophecy came true.

Although there are only a few stories of the nearby cemetery hosting a spirit, the mission itself is not haunted. Instead, it is said to give people an overwhelming experience of peace and tranquility when you enter. Perhaps this is caused by the beauty of the building alone, as it is truly one of the most fantastic and stunning landmarks around. At night, the gorgeous exterior is illuminated and can be seen from I-90.

The Cataldo Mission began in 1831, when the Nez Perce Indians headed east to meet with American explorer William Clark (1770–1838). The Jesuits came to the area around 1840s, but the Catholic missionaries didn't reach Idaho until 1842. The first mission was located near the St. Joe River thirty-five miles south of Cataldo but had to be relocated due to the floods prone to that land. Father Pierre-John DeSmet was called Chief of the Blackrobes by the local Indians.

This beautiful, historic church was designed by Father Antonio Ravalli, who was under Father DeSmet's command. The Italian born Jesuit priest

The Sacred Heart Mission in Cataldo in 1933. It looks quite different today. *Courtesy of Library of Congress, item no. id0020.*

fancied the Greek Revival style of buildings, and his dream of building a church in this style soon came to be a reality by using local supplies and the help of the large willing team of Coeur d'Alene Indians. Much labor and love went into the construction of the building, and Father Ravalli (1812–1884), an Italian Jesuit missionary, had great insight in his design. The church boasts a fantastic false Baroque-style gable, which makes it appear elaborate. The six heavy columns were made from the large trunks of local trees. Inside is exquisite, and the statues were carved by Father Ravalli himself. As it was limited in resources, the team became very creative in decorating the church. Team members decoratively cut tin cans to make chandeliers, the wallpaper is painted newsprint and the blue coloring on the wood was created by crushing huckleberries into the beams.

It is reported that Father Ravalli was inspired by a photograph he noticed in a book. The finished building is ninety feet long by forty feet wide and thirty feet high—without the use of a single nail. Working with only simple tools, building the church is nothing short of a miracle. In lieu of nails, Father Ravalli and the Indians made holes in the beams and inserted wood pegs into them to hold the pieces together. This was quite a task, considering this was completed during the years 1850 through 1853, when there was not a lot of equipment at hand.

Above: Visitors of the Cataldo Mission feel an overwhelming sense of happiness and relief. It holds a positive energy vortex. *Courtesy of Library of Congress, item no. id0020.*

Left: The beautiful wooden doors of the Cataldo Mission. Many say they feel a great sense of peace and love when entering the building. *Courtesy of author.*

Father Ravilli was known for developing a sensational relationship with the local Indians, who all adored and respected him. He welcomed them in every way and treated them with nothing but kindness and respect. Father Ravalli was trained in medicine as well.

A spiritual experience by the author:

> *If any building would have spirits roaming its rooms, the Cataldo Mission would be one of them. Although there seems to be no reports of the buildings being haunted, there are stories of people feeling an overwhelming sense of relief and love. I, too, experienced these overwhelmingly strong emotions on my visit. As soon as I walked through its thick, wooden double doors, I could feel a welcoming and uplifting feeling. At one point, I felt as if I was going to cry—not from sadness but from an unexplained feeling of joy. Several friends that were with me experienced the same emotions.*

Perhaps residual energy from the people who once worked so hard to build and promote the church still welcome visitors with open arms. It is uncertain why people who visit the old mission experience a sense of love and relief. One thing is certain: the beautiful building will be around for generations to enjoy due to the hard work and energy involved in restoring and protecting such a valuable piece of Idaho's history.

3

MURRAY

Gold in Them There Hills

Murray was founded in January 1884, and was formerly called Murrayville. Once a thriving gold town of five thousand residents, Murray has a small population of people living there today, but it still a fascinating and haunting place to visit. The town was named after George Murray, who was one of the first prospectors in the area. Andrew Jackson Prichard (1830–1902) originally came from Walla Walla, Washington, in search of a timber contract and was the first to discover gold in Murray in 1882. Known as the "Cradle City of the Coeur d'Alene's" in the late 1800s, Murray was a base camp for prospectors hoping to strike it rich. The gold rush in the area during the 1880s prompted men to flock to the nearby Eagle camp, which sprang up overnight (and was just as quickly abandoned in favor of nearby Murray) in the hopes of striking it rich. Even Wyatt Earp (1848–1929) was rumored to visit Murray with the news of the discovery of gold in the area. The later-famous fire ranger Edward Pulaski came to Murray in 1884 and was hired as a packer to run supplies over the treacherous pass for the merchant Saul Natham, who ran the first general store.

The cluster of small towns called Eagle City, Murray and Prichard soon reached a population of more than ten thousand people. Eagle City even caught the attention of the famous Wyatt Earp, his wife, Josie, and his brother James, and they quickly erected a large circus tent and ran it as the White Elephant Saloon. In 1898, they purchased the New Theater building for $132 and moved the White Elephant Saloon. It is recorded that the ghost town of Eagle City, during its productive years between

This 1888 wood engraving by Frederic Remington depicts men riding horseback in the Idaho mountains near Coeur d'Alene. *Courtesy of Library of Congress, item no. 2007677015.*

1883 and 1884, had thirty-eight lawyers, twenty-six stores, twenty-four hotels, eleven doctors and twenty-four saloons. Calamity Jane was in charge of organizing the first social and dance event in Eagle City. In old records housed in Shoshone County Courthouse in Wallace, the recorded documents show that Wyatt challenged several local claims, including those by local A.J. Prichard. Wyatt desired control of the claims named Consolidated Grizzly Bear, the Dividend, the Dead Scratch and the Golden Gate.

Wyatt purchased a cabin on Eagle Street, lot 57, from a man named William Buzard in May 1884. After the mini gold rush, Wyatt left town in a hurry for some reason and still owed back taxes of about ten dollars. Since Earp did lose his court battle against Prichard, it is a local legend that Wyatt was scheduled to be hung in Murray for mine claim jumping. No wonder the Earps left town in such a hurry.

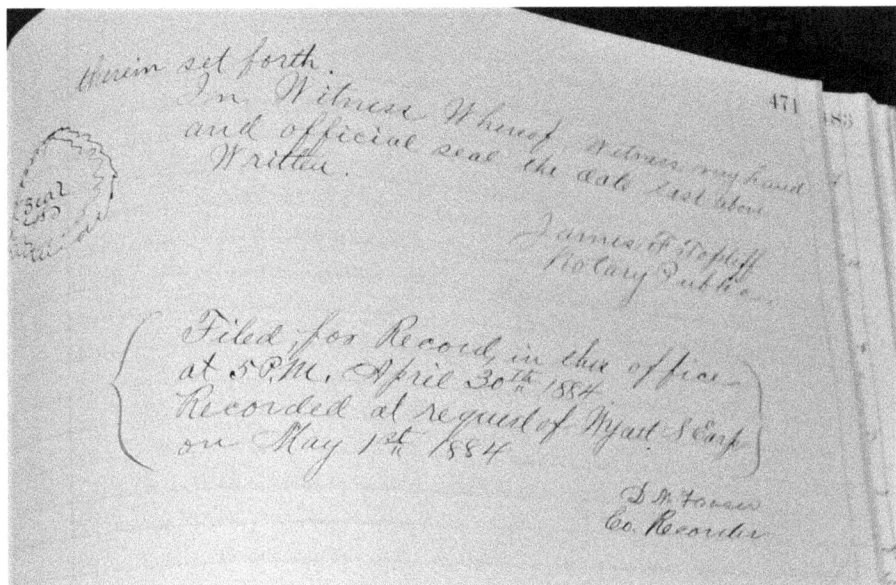

Wyatt Earp came to Idaho and challenged the claims of local A.J. Prichard. These were recorded in the courthouse in Murray. *Courtesy of author.*

In its heyday, Murray was booming with a whopping forty-four establishments that lined Main Street. Only a few of the original buildings remain today. The residents of Murray today truly embrace the old times of yesteryear and host a series of events, including Molly b'Damn days, which draw huge crowds each year.

Some locals seem unclear as to whether Wyatt Earp really landed for some time in Murray, Idaho, but records dated April 12, 1884 state:

> *Notice is hereby given to the undersigned have this day located twenty acres of Placer mining ground on hill side diggings situated in the Coeur d'Alene Mining District on the south side of Prichard Creek between Osburn and Murrayville Idaho territory.…I, Wyatt Earp, do solemnly swear that I am acquainted with the mining ground described in the notice of location herewith and that the ground and claim therein described, or any part thereof, has not to the best of my knowledge and belief been here to fore located accordingly to the laws of the United States and of this territory or if so located that the same has been abandoned or forfeited by reason of the failure of such former locators to comply in respect there to with the requirements of said laws.*
>
> *Signed Wyatt S. Earp, subscribed and sworn before me this 3rd day of April a.d. 1884.*

An unknown prospector in 1940. Both silver and gold can be found in Idaho. *Courtesy of Library of Congress, item no. 2017742232, photographer Russell Lee.*

Gold nuggets have been found as recently as 1998, when a road crew found a seven-ounce chunk. Like many of the mining towns in northern Idaho, once the fever is over, the town dries up and people move away. Several of the original 1884 buildings remain in Murray, including the Murray House Bed-and-Breakfast, the Sprag Pole Inn and the Bedroom Goldmine Bar. All are reported to be haunted.

Several of the locals claim spirits from Murray's lively past help keep the town alive today.

MURRAY HOUSE BED-AND-BREAKFAST

A ghost story from Sandy, owner of the Murray House:

> *Although we have never felt a negative presence or anything scary, we do hear walking from above almost every night at 9:00 p.m. in the A.J. Prichard room. When experimenting with dowsing rods, I asked the question, "Is there any silver in the house?" and the rods pointed directly*

to the silver we had on display. Another time, when in the Adam Aulbach room, I asked, "Adam are you here?" The rods went crazy. When I asked, "Where are you?" they pointed to a nearby chair. Then I felt my left arm go ice cold, so I asked again, "Adam, where are you?" And the rods pointed to my left side. We had two mediums visit the Murray House, and they both agreed the house has a good aura and is very welcoming and peaceful. I was taking photographs of the rooms for our website, and in one photo, it looks like there is wind blowing through the room and what is clearly an image of Adam Aulbach's face. His big nose, thick moustache and down-turned mouth are spot on when you compare his ghost image with his living photograph.

The friendly spirit who is said to haunt the Murray House Bed-and-Breakfast is the original owner himself, Adam Aulbach (1844–1933), who lived in the house until his death. Aulbach was born in Belleville, Illinois, on Christmas day. His parents were from Germany. In his forties, Aulbach made his way to northern Idaho, dragging his newspaper and printing equipment all the way from Trout Creek, Montana, with the use of forty-five mules. Aulbach

The Murray House Bed-and-Breakfast is haunted by its original owner, Adam Aulbach, and the spirit of a little girl. *Courtesy of author.*

Right: Adam Aulbach haunts the Murray House Bed-and-Breakfast. Aulbach was a pillar in the town of Murray. *Courtesy of Sandy Hammer, owner of Murray House.*

Below: Aulbach's ghostly face can be seen in this photograph. *Courtesy of Sandy Hammer, owner of Murray House.*

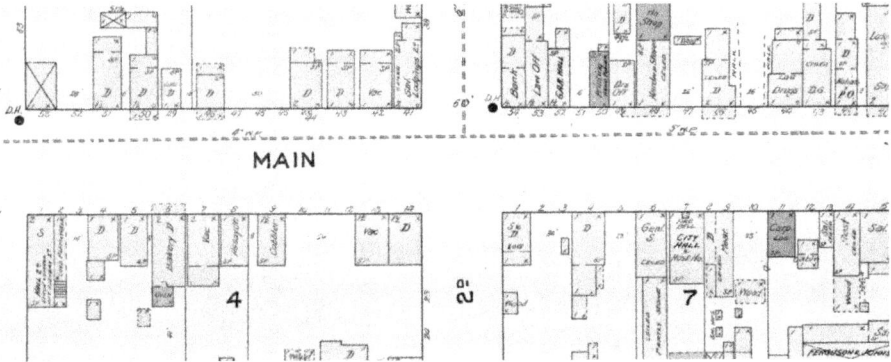

Sanborn fire insurance map for Murray from 1896, showing Burten's Bakery at lot no. 6 (*bottom left*). *Courtesy of Library of Congress, item no. sanborn01643_001.*

quickly set up shop in Murray and ran his first edition of the *Idaho Sun* on July 8, 1884. He married Rose Zaugg (1862–1947) on February 5, 1888.

Aulbach was a key player for the small town, and he had his hand in almost everything from supplying water to developing the first volunteer fire department. He built Murray's first electric light plant in 1910. He earned the name the "Grand Old Man of Murray." Aulbach also had five claims, but the Buckeye Boy Mine was his pride and joy. Aulbach served in the Civil War and later became the mayor of Murray. At eighty-eight years old, Aulbach died on June 9, 1933, in his home in Murray, with his loving daughter, Ruth Sellers, by his side. The Buckeye Mine is the final resting place of Aulbach, as his ashes are spread in the beautiful mountains near his beloved mine. *The Miner* reported on January 7, 1909, "There is not a better citizen more loyal to the Coeur d'Alene region than Adam Aulbach."

Adam Aulbach was a well-loved local and was always highly respected in Murray. It is no wonder that he refuses to leave his treasured town and his well-loved and beautiful home. Adam originally rented out the right side of the home for his newspaper, and the other side was a bank owned by Warren Hussey. Adam was eventually able to purchase the entire home.

Is the spirit of a little girl seen in the home by a prior owner the young spirit of his daughter, Ruth, when she was a child? Can ghosts come back at a different age than when they actually died? It has been suggested that ghosts can return appearing as the age they liked best during their living years. Some ghosts appear youthful and healthy, even when they suffered from disease in the last portion of their lives.

The apparition of Adam Aulbach has been captured in a photograph taken inside the home—the facial image clearly that of Aulbach, with his thick moustache, down-turned mouth and round nose. There is no mistaking the ghost for anyone else—the characteristics are too clear to be ignored. Aulbach still resides in his favorite place in the world. The Murray House Bed-and-Breakfast, although it has been renovated and updated, still carries charm and interesting details from the past. An old bank window can be seen from the lobby, and many old relics, photographs and artifacts have been preserved by the current owners, Larry and Sandy Hammer. Stay in one of their elegant and comfortable rooms for the weekend, and maybe the spirit of the little girl or Adam Aulbach will appear.

BEDROOM GOLDMINE BAR

A ghost story from the current owner, Chris Littlejohn:

I tend to open up the bar early. I often hear footsteps when no one else is in here. I also hear things moving around, and I think to myself, "That's too loud to be a mouse." My bartender, Kimmy, also has experienced things such as icy cold drafts and doors opening and closing by themselves.

Is it possible that one of the old prospectors doesn't want anyone else getting their hands on their gold at the Bedroom Goldmine Bar? One of the oldest and original buildings in Murray, the Bedroom Goldmine has an interesting history that can't be ignored. Originally built in 1884, a man named E.W. Burten opened a bakery there, which blossomed into a general store.

The grave marker for E.W. Buren, who owned a bakery in the building that is now the haunted Bedroom Goldmine Bar. *Courtesy of author.*

Chris (1910–1999) and Lucille (1913–1999) Christopherson moved to Murray in 1962. Around 1967, the Christophersons purchased the general store and decided to turn it into a tavern. Chris was always dreaming of finding gold, so while his wife tended the bar, he (not wanting to deal with the cold weather) decided to dig a shaft 34 feet into the ground in protected elements. He dug an incredible 120 feet of drift tunnels too. Where did he decide to dig his own personal shaft? In an unused bedroom in the back of the building. Chris figured that since his building was one of the few remaining original buildings in town, maybe there was gold hidden beneath its floor.

Much to his wife's dismay, Chris continued to search for gold in his private indoor mine. While locals were shaking their heads and whistling between their teeth, the final joke was on them in the late 1960s, as Chris did find gold in his mine shaft—one of the biggest nuggets ever to be found in the Coeur d'Alene's. The eight-and-a-half-ounce nugget brought much pleasure to the Christophersons.

At age eighty-one, Chris had enough of digging and gave it up. He stopped working his mine in 1982. He would tell locals, "I'm not going to do any more digging 'til I get to Heaven." Some wonder if it is Chris's spirit who now haunts the bar. Is he still searching for more gold?

In 1988, Chris gave the bar to his niece, Leila Grebil (1940–2017), and her husband, Frank (1923–2000). Nobody knew that building better than Leila, as she had been working there since 1965. For several decades Frank

The haunted Bedroom Goldmine Bar in Murray attracts visitors from far away for both its food and fascinating history. *Courtesy of author.*

Frank Grebil is reportedly the friendly spirit who haunts the bar, which he used to own. *Courtesy of Chris Littlejohn, owner.*

was known to take his sons, Greg Grebil and Mike Lavergne, into the mine with him to search for gold. They would haul debris and rocks back up in a five-gallon plastic bucket. They had an old bathtub behind the building where they would put the overburden (miscellaneous material), and visitors and customers could then pan for gold in it. And, better yet, they got to keep any gold they found.

Unfortunately, in 1996, there was a terrible storm in Murray, and the whole town was flooded, causing a lot of problems for the locals. Parts of the Grebils' mine and tunnel collapsed. As the shaft and tunnel slowly filled with water, the fun of working the mine went with it, and for safety reasons, the mine was closed. The shaft was shored up and strengthened and then covered with a clear floor section to preserve the fascinating history of the mine for future generations to enjoy.

While alive, Frank's favorite stool was placed directly in front of a large, wooden beam. He would always rest his back against it. Some think it is the spirit of Frank who haunts the place, not Chris. After his death, when the front door would fly open, customers would ask, "Who is that?" Leila would joke that it was Frank coming in to sit at his favorite bar stool.

In 2007, Leila sold the bar to new owners, Tammie and Barry Gleason, who began an extensive, three-year remodel. The building had a mean lean to the east, and people could even see light from the passing cars through the wooden slats. During the remodel, Frank's beam had to be moved. Employees and owners claim that since the beam has been moved, the door no longer swings open for no reason like it did before. Has the spirit of Frank vanished, or is he mad about his beam being moved? They do still report the sound of footsteps walking in the bar when no one else is in the room. But they would like to think that it is Frank, still popping in to say hello and pass some time at his favorite place.

A ghost story from Kim Grebil:

> *Over the past thirty-one years I've worked at the Goldmine Bar, I've heard and seen a few things about the bar and whether or not it is actually*

haunted by the spirits of the past and my late father-in-law coming to reclaim his favorite bar stool or maybe just stories from customers who have had too much of the spirits we sell off our top shelf….As for me, personally, I would like to think that it's the former and I am surrounded by my friends and family who have passed on and are coming here to check on me and visit their once favorite watering hole. And so, when it's late at night and everyone has gone home and I am closing the bar and a cool breeze washed over me and I hear that now-familiar faint sound of footsteps, instead of thinking it is just the wind, I choose to believe it is my mother and father-in-law dancing across the floor to their favorite song on the jukebox.

Kim Grebil, Leila's daughter-in-law, has been working there since she was sixteen years old and has had a few friendly ghostly encounters as well. Kim and Greg Grebil are now married, and they have spent most of their lives at the Bedroom Goldmine Bar and down in the old mine, and if you stop in, they have lots of great stories to share.

After several years and changing of owners, the current Bedroom Goldmine Bar owners, Tammie and Chris Littlejohn, finally owned the bar—a dream they both shared. They love the little town of Murray and all of its history. They love that Wyatt Earp probably stopped into the old building when it was a bakery or general store back in the day. More than likely, Molly b'Damn even sauntered through the building for merchandise or a cup of coffee when she lived in Murray.

Today, the place is known for its pizza, the fantastic history and the friendly atmosphere. Tammie and Chris have made their dreams a reality and continue to make the locals and tourists feel right at home. They have a great love for cooking and setting up for local functions and festivals that bring people together for a fun time. When they took over the bar, some main obstacles were getting the kitchen and food storage areas up to par and developing a much larger menu than the Bedroom Goldmine had before. That took time and money but was well worth the effort.

Although some may find living in the small town of Murray a bit out of the way, Tammie and Chris feel it is a truly a dream come true for them. Murray is a small-town community with a small-town atmosphere. People living there are happy and friendly—perhaps that is why the lingering spirits don't want to leave such a wonderful place.

The opening of the original shaft is still there today, covered by a thick glass, and people can peer down the deep thirty-four-foot hole that was once just a local man's dream of finding gold. People stop in and look down the

Greg Grebil (*left*) and an unidentified man working in the mine at the Bedroom Goldmine shaft. *Courtesy of Chris Littlejohn, owner.*

Peering into the shaft at the Bedroom Goldmine Bar, where a huge gold nugget was found by Chris Christopherson. *Courtesy of author.*

old opening and nervously hope to see a ghost or two looking back up at them. And if while there the front door blows open for no reason at all, everyone turns their head and hopes that it is the good old spirit of Frank coming back to sit at his favorite stool. Perhaps someday his ghost will be captured on a security tape or in a photograph.

Until then, Frank Grebil's ghost simply comes and goes as it pleases, making the locals happy that he still hangs around them at the Bedroom Goldmine Bar and his old mine.

ALTHOUGH IT IS NOT reported to be haunted, the beautiful and historic Masonic hall located to the left of the Bedroom Goldmine Bar is worth a mention. It is one of the few remaining original structures in Murray. Built in 1884, it is the oldest-running Masonic hall in Idaho. In 1886, Adam Aulbach (ghost of the Murray House Bed-and-Breakfast) donated the building to the Masons Association. On the original document for the lodge, the word "State" has been crossed out and the word "Territory" has been written in its place because at that time, Idaho was not yet a state. Some of the original details from the old days are still there, including the historic wallpaper and some of the furnishings.

SPRAG POLE INN AND MUSEUM

The historic building was constructed in 1884, and it was known as the J.R. Marks Hardware Store. It is one of the few remaining original buildings in the almost ghost town from that era. In 1885, it became the Murray Express Office and stagecoach stop. It is unclear how the building was used until 1933, when a man named Walt Almquist (1909–2000) bought the place. Walt and his wife, Bess, lovingly ran the restaurant called the Sprag Pole Inn for several decades. When Walt was given an old whiskey jug from his friend Lyle Wurm in the early 1970s, Walt had a wild brainstorm. He wanted to build a museum in the adjoining structure, the Murray Building, and create a collection of artifacts and curios for people to enjoy. After securing the purchase of the building, his plan was set in motion. Excited at the thought of a new adventure, his brother Harry soon wanted in on the fun. The two set out to form a one-of-a-kind eclectic, amusing and fascinating museum unlike anything anywhere around—and that they did.

The Sprag Pole Inn is one of the few remaining original buildings left in the town of Murray. *Courtesy of author.*

The ten-thousand-square-foot museum was slowly put together by Walt, his family and members of the community. Glass cases were built to house collections. His nephew Glen got to work setting up the mining and logging exhibits, as well as the doctor's office display.

The must-see museum boasts twelve special exhibits, including an acclaimed mining exhibit; replicas of an old blacksmith shop; an old-fashioned school room; a furnished parlor; a replicated 1900s kitchen; an old post office; many Native Indians artifacts; a collection of logging, forestry and firefighting pieces; and an expansive rock and mineral display. It also has war memorabilia, hundreds of small hand-carved animals that Walt created, old electronics, old bottles and much more. It even houses the world's largest hand-carved wooden chain. An antique wooden barber pole from 1900 stands with a sign advising visitors that it was used by local barber Robert Skeman Sr., back in the old days.

In one area, there is a mockup of Molly b'Damn's bedroom, complete with her original tombstone.

Note: This is located at 6353 Prichard Street in Murray. Although the museum is a nonprofit and offers free admission, donations are welcome, as the building needs some repairs. Please help keep this historic building available for future generations to enjoy.

MOLLY B'DAMN AND CALAMITY JANE MEET

Molly b'Damn: a local legend

Molly b'Damn (1853–1888), whose real name was Maggie Hall, was a high-spirited and well-educated prostitute who turned into a local heroine during a local smallpox epidemic. She was known to be a caring and nurturing individual. Born on December 26, 1853, in Dublin, Ireland, the legendary Molly b'Damn came to the United States at age twenty in 1873. Fleeing from the residual results of the famine that plagued Ireland in 1845 (the failed potato crops led to the deaths of about 750,000 people), Molly was one of many to head to New York to start a new life. A year later, she married a man named Burdan, and for some reason, she changed her first name to Molly. Tiring of her husband's antics, Molly left him and traveled the states in search of her next adventure. During one of her travels, she met up with another famous Wild West woman, Calamity Jane.

Molly came to Murray in 1884 and became a business owner, taking up Cabin no. 1—the madam's residence. Although she ran a brothel, she was very considerate of her new community and immediately became well loved by everyone. It was told that she could quote Shakespeare, Dante and Milton. Molly tirelessly tended to anyone who was in need or sick, always thinking of others before herself. But this selflessness would be the death of her as she contracted tuberculosis after caring for many others who had contracted the dreaded disease. In 1888, Molly succumbed and died with many people at her side. The funeral brought over a thousand people to pay their respects to Molly—the "Patron Saint of Murray."

Molly b'Damn was one of the most well-known female figures of the Coeur d'Alene region. Some think her ghost still roams the streets of her

Molly b'Damn's original grave marker is housed at the museum. Locals like to think the loving spirit of Molly still roams her favorite town. *Courtesy of author.*

hometown. Paranormal activists try to capture her voice on recorders in the small cemetery nearby. Others think she haunts the Sprag Pole Museum, where her original tombstone resides.

Many paranormal investigators walk among the pioneer graves at the nearby GAR Cemetery where she lies, hoping to capture an EVP from her (or any ghost!) or a spike on their equipment signaling activity.

The town hosts its Molly b'Damn days on the second weekend in August—a three-day bash of contests, vendors, music and festivities. Perhaps Molly herself will grace the street with her apparition.

Calamity Jane: A Wild West Legend

Calamity Jane (1852–1903), whose real name was Martha Jane Canary Burke, was recorded traveling the West, mostly following the Northern Pacific Railroad routes. She was in Livingston, Montana, when she heard the news about finding gold in Idaho. Calamity was known to frequent northern Idaho on her many travels and lived in the Coeur d'Alene/Spokane region in the early 1900s, while dealing a card game called faro. She had earned quite the reputation working at a little saloon on Main Avenue in Spokane, which was adjacent to the Owl Saloon. Calamity was lifelong pals with the legendary Wild Bill Hickok, and in 1876, they rode into Deadwood, South Dakota, together, along with many others heading that way. Unfortunately, Wild Bill was shot and died soon thereafter while playing poker. On August 2, Hickok was playing poker in the Nuttal & Mann's Saloon located at 624 Main Street. A disgruntled man named Jack McCall snuck up behind Hickok and shot him in the back of the head, killing him instantly. He fell to the floor holding a pair of aces and a pair of eights—now known as the "dead man's hand." Although acquitted at first, McCall was later found guilty and hanged for the murder. He claimed that he killed Hickok because Hickok had killed his brother in Abilene, Kansas. Calamity was heartbroken over the loss of her friend and vowed to be buried next to him when it was her time to go. Calamity died in Terry, South Dakota, on August 1, 1903. Her desire to be buried next to Wild Bill came true.

The *Evening Standard* on May 6, 1911, summed up Calamity when it published: "Men would follow her into any danger. She could handle a rifle, a revolver or knife with the skill of an expert, rode a vicious mustang and seemed utterly without the sense of fear. In short, she was a woman only in sex, a man in mind, heart, muscle and courage."

Above: The graves of James Butler "Wild Bill" Hickok and Martha "Calamity Jane" Burke at Mount Moriah Cemetery in Deadwood, South Dakota. *Courtesy of Joshua Davis.*

Left: Martha Jane Burke, popularly known as Calamity Jane, holding a rifle in 1895. *Courtesy of Library of Congress, item no. 2016651866, photographer H.R. Locke.*

Two Famous Wild West Women Meet

In 1884, Molly met Calamity Jane on a train headed to Thompson Falls, Idaho, in February 1884. Both were interested in the recent gold discovery in the Coeur d'Alene mountains. It was well known that Calamity Jane was an excellent shot, had won many duels and was not afraid of anything. A year earlier, Calamity saved the life of a cavalry officer named Captain John F. Egan (1898–1996), who was about to be scalped by local Indians. Somehow, Calamity was able to scare the tribesmen off, and Egan's life was saved. She hoisted the captain's unconscious body across her horse and rode back to the safety of the camp. When Egan regained consciousness, he heard of what had happened and was so moved by her feat that it was written in the *Tonopah Bonanza* on August 22, 1903, that Egan said, "You are a good person to have around in times of calamity, and I christen you Calamity Jane, the heroine of the plains!" Although other stories exist, Egan was supposedly the one responsible for the nickname.

In February 1884, Molly traveled by a horse and mule caravan on the Thompson Falls Pass toward the Coeur d'Alenes. Although at one time she desired to go to the Coeur d'Alenes, Calamity did not follow Molly into Murray but instead headed toward Spokane. Perhaps Calamity Jane should have proceeded on to Murray in search of gold, as it was noted in the *Coeur d'Alene Nugget* on April 9, 1884:

> *Calamity Jane, the most noted woman of the Western frontier and the heroine of many a thrilling nickel novel, has pulled up stakes and joined the stampede for Coeur d'Alene. The above item has been going the rounds and the Belknap Enterprise gives the following sequel....The only genuine and original Calamity Jane of Black Hills fame has arrived in town last Wednesday night. She was penniless, not even able to pay for her lodging, but began work as a restaurant cook next morning. It was a big card for the restaurant as many had a desire to see the charming old lady.*

Molly's group trekked through the deep snow on the trails with a nasty blizzard forming as they rode along. During the ride, Molly discovered a shivering woman with her small child sitting in the snow, almost freezing to death. No one else had stopped to help the woman and child, although many took note of Molly's kindness to the female stranger as they pressed on. The three piled onto Molly's horse and headed a bit farther down the trail until they came on a small shelter, where they decided to camp for the night and warm themselves by a fire. Molly wrapped the strangers in her extra coats, ultimately saving both of their lives.

The next morning, Molly, the woman and child rode into the small town of Murray, Idaho, where she was fondly addressed by many people who considered her brave and selfless—a new town heroine.

In Murray, she introduced herself to a local man named Phil O'Rourke, who took a liking to her, but with her thick Irish accent, her name sound like Molly *b'Damn* instead of Molly *Burdan*, thus her new nickname was created. Molly felt right at home in Murray and decided to stay. She eventually opened her own saloon nearby, called the Acion Saloon, and she acquired several lots in town. Wyatt Earp's wife, Josie, often took to singing at the Acion Saloon. One of Molly's famous acts was to bask in a bathtub in the middle of Main Street in Murray and have the prospectors toss money and gold flecks at her in exchange for washing her back. Molly also became well known for being a kind and caring resident. In December 1885, she sold the Acion Saloon lot to a woman named Mrs. C.R. Boyce.

When the dreaded tuberculosis hit the small town of Murray in 1886, Molly wasted no time tending to the sick. Unfortunately, her kindness did not shelter her from getting tuberculosis herself a year later. Her final words were, "My real name is Maggie Hall. It was the name of my mother. She was a wonderful and good woman." She died with several people at her side on January 17, 1888, and it is said that over one thousand people followed her casket loaded onto a four-horse wagon all the way through town, each mourning the death of a much-loved local woman.

Unfortunately, there are no known photographs of Molly b'Damn, although it is recorded that she was beautiful and well kept. The town named its favorite annual festival the Molly b'Damn Gold Rush Days in her honor, and people come from all over to enjoy the three-day jubilee. Molly b'Damn is buried in the local cemetery just a mile or so from town. Does her spirit still roam the small town she grew to love so much, her kindness still warming the hearts of the people who live there? Many ghost hunters have tried to contact the spirit of Molly b'Damn in the local cemetery. Maybe she haunts the Sprag Pole Museum where her original tombstone can be seen in one of the exhibits.

4

KELLOGG

A Town Rich in History

Ghosts have a way of misleading you;
they can make your thoughts as heavy as branches after a storm.
——Rebecca Maizel

The Silver Valley Mountains have been giving up their riches for as long as men have dug through their hard surfaces. Millions of dollars' worth of lead, silver and even some gold have made many men extremely wealthy and have driven others to poverty, madness and even suicide. The mountains still hold tons of valuable products, even though many of the mines have been shut down or decommissioned.

The small mining town of Kellogg was named after Noah Spencer Kellogg (1831–1903), who was famous for locating (with the help of his borrowed donkey) the productive Bunker Hill lode. The Bunker Hill mine and smelter at one time employed 2,500 people and had the nickname "Uncle Bunker," because it helped pay for many of the town amenities. Kellogg, a carpenter by trade, came to the nearby area of Eagle City in 1884 at age fifty-five, with five dollars, a few clothes and his bedroll. When the five dollars ran out, he borrowed sixteen dollars from E.D. Garrison and headed to another small town called Murray. He worked odd jobs to get by, but Kellogg soon fell on hard times and became penniless.

In 1884, he had the idea of building a shingle mill, but the equipment was not of the right caliber, and the mill never produced any shingles. Kellogg was known to always pay off any debts and was known as a kind and

Unidentified miners work deep underground in the Coeur d'Alene region of Idaho in 1909. *Courtesy of Library of Congress, item no. 96515275.*

reasonable man. He decided to try his luck at finding gold or silver in the mountains. He persuaded a local doctor named Cooper and a contractor named Origin Peck to loan him money for thirty-five pounds of bacon, ten pounds of beans, fifteen pounds of flour, some sugar and some coffee. Kellogg packed his supplies on the back of the loose burro running around town and set off to find his fortune. Kellogg was a big believer in the spirit world, and it is said that he often saw visions that came true. Before his lucky find that eventually became Bunker Hill, he told people that he had a vision of the mountainside opening up to reveal big veins of silver and gold. For four hours, he laid in his bed thinking about the possibility of finding a fortune in the hills—a vision that later came true. Bunker Hill would become the world's largest silver mine.

THE MILLION-DOLLAR JACKASS

The legend of the million-dollar donkey is well known in Kellogg. As the story is told, the borrowed jackass wandered off in the middle of the night, and Kellogg had to follow his trail by looking for tufts of donkey hair caught on branches and stumps. When Kellogg finally located the missing donkey, they were standing on opposite sides of the creek. He called for the donkey, but the animal ignored him and continued to stare at something in the grass. Frustrated, Kellogg went to retrieve the donkey. He bent down to see what the donkey was looking at. Lo and behold, the animal was staring at a big vein of lead and silver.

In 1885, the mine sold for $1.5 million, and by 1910, the mine had produced $12,031,500. A legal battle ensued between the original burro owners, Cooper & Peck, Kellogg, his partner Phil O'Rouke and the donkey. Eventually, the judge ruled in favor of the latter group. Kellogg later said, "Men may say what they choose, but if not for that dumb beast the Bunker-Hill Mine would not have been discovered by me!" The burro was not dumb at all, in fact he became a legend. The donkey was described as "a Spanish jackass with a head nearly as big as his body, ears so long that when he laid them back they touched his withers and he was extremely cunning and tricky."

SUNSHINE MINE DISASTER

On a tragic day on May 2, 1972, 173 miners eagerly went to work in the Sunshine Mine located between Kellogg and Wallace, yet only 82 of them would return to their families that day. Unfortunately, the other 91 men died of carbon monoxide poisoning. The last of the men trapped, Tom Wilkinson and Ron Flory, stared death in the eyes until May 9 (175 very long, nerve-racking hours later), when they were finally rescued.

The town of Kellogg was originally platted and filed as "Milo" on July 1, 1893, but in 1894, the citizens chose to change its name to Kellogg in honor of Noah Kellogg. Once one of the largest silver mines in the United States, the Sunshine was claimed by two brothers, True and Dennis Blake, in 1884. The brothers had come to Big Creek from Maine in 1880. In Big Creek, they discovered ore deposits and claimed the Yankee Lode. Later, in 1921, a twenty-five-ton-per-day mill was built and up to five hundred tons per day was extracted. In 1942, the Chester vein was discovered.

Since 1904, the Sunshine Mine has produced 364,893,421 ounces of silver and millions more tons of lead, ore and copper. After many years of making men rich, a horrible disaster struck at the Sunshine Mine, leaving the

Left: The memorial in honor of the ninety-one men who died in the Sunshine Mine disaster on May 2, 1972, in Kellogg. *Courtesy of author.*

Below: A drawing of the sections and shafts at the Sunshine Mine. The area marked is where the tragic fire started. *Courtesy of the U.S. Department of the Interior, Bureau of Mines.*

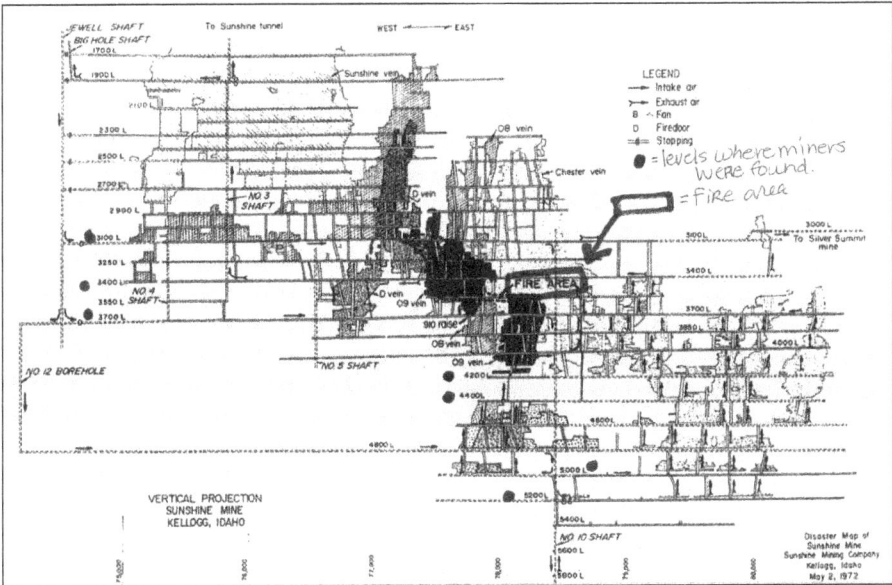

occupation of mining to never be the same. The Sunshine miners accessed the mine by walking to the Jewell shaft (top left on map) and were hoisted down to the 3,100 and 3,700 levels and then moved by a small train to the no. 10 shaft (extended from 3,100 to 6,000 feet), where they would go even lower into the ground until they ended up at their appropriate levels and were stationed to work.

Deep down in the depths of the earth where most men would never dare to go, these men descended every day without batting an eye at the danger that always lurked below.

One morning, danger won. Thirty-one men were trapped at the 3,100 level, twenty-one men were at the 5,200 level, sixteen at the 3,700 level, seven at the 4,400 level, four at the 3,400 level, three at the 4,200 level and two at the 5,000 level. At 11:40 a.m., smoke was discovered at the 910 raise on the 3,700 level. At about 12:03 p.m., the evacuation process had begun, but it was not quick enough. The lethal carbon monoxide quickly pushed its way through the sections, dangerously surging its way up the main airways. Most exits were soon blocked by a thick smoke, making some escape routes useless. A brave man worked the hoist, bringing up

Several unidentified miners working with candlelight during the early 1900s. *Courtesy of Library of Congress, photographer S.A. Noyes.*

The numbered tags are an easy way to keep track of miners—who is on shift and if they are inside the mine. *Courtesy of author.*

men to safety, until he finally succumbed to the gases and died. The fire was determined to be started by spontaneous combustion of scrap timbers. The last victim was removed from the mine on May 13. Many people still visit the memorial today in honor of the men who tragically lost their lives that day.

A ghost story from Suzanne in Wallace:

> *I decided to stop and visit the Sunshine Miners Memorial one morning on my way to Kellogg, and I saw a woman standing by the statue of the miner. She looked incredibly sad. I thought to myself, I wonder if she is one of the widows of one of the men who died that day in the mine fire....It was no sooner that I thought this, that she disappeared. Unless she walked away really fast, although I did not see her anywhere else nor another car, I have no explanation for the woman I thought I saw. When I told my friend the story, she thought maybe it was the ghost of one of the women who lost her husband and she was also visiting the memorial to honor her lost love.*

Above: The plaque at the Sunshine Memorial lists the names of the ninety-one men who died in the fire in 1972. *Courtesy of author.*

Right: A horse and unidentified miners working three miles underground in 1895. *Courtesy of Library of Congress, item no. 2015646069, photograph by Strohmeyer & Wyman.*

On researching the group of victims, I was terribly sad to note how many young men in their teens lost their lives, as well as many father-son duos working at the Sunshine mine during the disaster. So many wives, mothers, grandmothers, girlfriends, friends and neighbors lost their loved ones that horrible day. It would be almost impossible to determine who the female spirit could be roaming the memorial, as so many women's worlds were ripped apart. Rest in peace, all of the brave and hardworking men who perished in the tragedy. Much respect and honor also goes to the incredible men who risked their lives during and after the fire in their heroic rescue efforts.

Victims of the Sunshine Mine Disaster May 2, 1972

(Name, age, hometown, occupation)

Robert H. Alexander, 50, Kellogg, Stope Miner
Billy W. Allen, 24, Big Creek, Raise Miner
Wayne L. Allen, 39, Big Creek, Drift Miner
Richard Marlin Allison, 37, Wallace, Drift Miner
Arnold Evert Anderson, 48, Wardner, Electrician
Robert Lewis Anderson, 37, Osburn, Boss
Joe E. Armijo, 38, Wallace, Stope Miner
Benjamin S. Barber, 31, Kellogg, Repairman.
Robert E. Barker, 42, Kellogg, Shaft Repairman
Virgil F. Bebb, 53, Montgomery Gulch, Shift Boss
Donald G. Beehner, 38, Wallace, Nipper
Richard D. Bewley, 40, Kellogg, Motorman
George W. Birchett, 40, Smelterville, Stope Miner
Wayne Blalack, 35, Cataldo, Electrician
Robert A. Bush, 47, Kellogg, Foreman
Floyd L. Byington, 35, Moon Gulch, Stope Miner
Clarence Lee Case, 55, Mullan, Shift Boss
Charles L. Casteel, 30, Osburn, Shift Boss
Kevin Alfred Croker, 29, Wallace, Repairman
Duwain D. Crow, 39, Big Creek, Drift Miner
Roderick B. Davenport, 35, Pinehurst, Stope Miner
John W. Davis, 28, Wallace, Diamond Driller
Richard L. Delbridge, 24, Osburn, Stope Miner
William R. Delbridge, 55, Wallace, Stope Miner
Roberto Diaz, 55, Mullen, Motorman

Gregory G. Dionne, 23, Hayden Lake, Pipeman
Carter M. Don Carlos, 47, Black Lake, Repairman
Norman S. Fee, 27, Wallace, Motor Helper
Lyle M. Findley, 30, Kellogg, Repairman
Donald K. Firkins, 37, Pinehurst, Drift Miner
Howard L. Fleshman, 38, Pinehurst, Stope Miner
William L. Follette, 23, Harrison, Raise Miner
Richard Garcia, 56, Kellogg, Stope Miner
Richard Glen George, 20, Wallace, Motor Helper
Robert W. Goff, 35, Osburn, Stope Miner
Louis W. Goos, 51, Wallace, Raise Miner
John P. Guertner, 54, Osburn, Repairman
William F. Hanna, 47, Kellogg, Pumpman
Howard Harrison, 34, Osburn, Drift Miner
Patrick Michael Hobson, 57, Kellogg, Repairman
Melvin Leroy House, 41, Wallace, Repairman
Merle E. Hudson, 47, Kellogg, Stope Miner
Jack B. Ivers, 44, Kellogg, Stope Miner
Fred E. Johnson, 45, Big Creek, Foreman
Paul Eugene Johnson, 47, Kingston, Shift Boss
Wayne L. Johnson, 43, Post Falls, Repairman
James Michael Johnston, 20, Coeur d'Alene, Motor Helper
Custer L. Keough, 59, Osburn, Repairman
Sherman C. Kester, 60, Big Creek, Trackman
Dewellyn E. Kitchen, 31, Coeur d'Alene, Stope Miner
Elmer E. Kitchen, 54, Coeur d'Alene, Shaft Miner
Kenneth Charles Lavoie, 29, Kingston, Repairman
Richard M. Lynch, 24, Osburn, Motorman
Donald J. Mclachlan, 23, Kellogg, Motorman
Delbert J. Mcnutt, 48, Enaville, Motorman
James Charles Moore, 29, Pinehurst, Repairman
David Jerry Mullin, 34, Pinehurst, Stope Miner
Joseph R. Naccarato, 40, Osburn, Raise Miner
Orlin Wayne Nelson, 32, Osburn, Stope Miner
Richard Dale Norris, 24, Smelterville, Raise Miner
Donald R. Orr, 50, Big Creek, Stope Miner
Hubert B. Patrick, 45, Kellogg, Drift Miner
Casey Pena, 52, Mullan, Shaft Miner
John W. Peterson, 57, Wallace, Motorman

Francis W. Phillips, 42, Kellogg, Repairman
Irvin L. Puckett, 51, Spokane, Shaft Repairman
Floyd A. Rais, 61, Kellogg, Pumpman
Leonard Dale Rathbun, 29, Wallace, Stope Miner
John R. Rawson, 27, Osburn, Drift Miner
Jack L. Reichert, 45, Big Creek, Hoistman
Delbert C. "Dusty" Rhoads, 57, Big Creek, Lead Mechanic
Glen R. Rossiter, 37, Wallace, Motorman
Paul M. Russell, 30, Kellogg, Stope Miner
Gene F. Salyer, 54, Kellogg, Repairman
James P. Salyer, 51, Kellogg, Foreman
Allan L. Sargent, 38, Rose Lake, Drift Miner
Robert B. Scanlan, 38, Wallace, Hoistman
John Raul Serano, 37, Smelterville, Stope Miner
Nick D. Sharette, 48, Osburn, Shaft Miner
Frank R. Sisk, 31, Kellogg, Stope Miner
Darrell E. Stephens, 20, Wallace, Motor Helper
Gustav G. Thor, 38, Pinehurst, Stope Miner
Grady D. Truelock, 40, Moon Gulch, Raise Miner
Robert E. Waldvogel, 50, Kellogg, Stope Miner
William Roy Walty, 29, Pinehurst, Repairman
Gordon Whatcott, 37, Kellogg, Stope Miner
Douglas Lee Wiederrick, 37, Mullan, Shaft Miner
Ronald L. Wilson, 41, Osburn, Drift Miner
William E. Wilson, 28, Coeur D'alene, Hoistman
John D. Wolff, 49, Kingston, Stope Miner
Don B. Wood, 53, Osburn, Hoistman

Stope Miner: A method to remove ore, other minerals or waste debris to create an open space, cave or room.
Raise Miner: Creates a vertical shaft that leads from one level to another.
Drift Miner: Cut/portal into the side of the bank or Earth horizontally.
Nipper: A helper, sometimes a new or beginning miner, makes sure there are proper supplies and materials.
Pipeman: Utilities, lays and repairs pipes that handle compressed air, steam or water and ventilation.
Motor Helper: Assists the motorman, empties cars.
Pumpman: Drill doctor—operates and repairs the pumps, drilling and pumping machinery.

Motorman: Operates the motor in the haulage of mine cars, locomotive engineer.

Hoistman: Operates the hoist, raises and lowers men, supplies, materials in and out of the mine.

TWO MILLION IN BURIED GOLD NEAR KELLOGG

If a spirit roams the area near Kellogg, it is to find their lost gold.

One anonymous person told the author a story of seeing ghosts dressed in period attire from days long ago:

> *I want to remain anonymous, because some people might think I am making stuff up or that I am crazy. Neither of those things are true. I can see spirits or ghosts, whatever you want to call them. A few times I have seen ghosts walking on the side of the highway, on I-90. They are always dressed in clothes from another era. I see the spirit of a younger girl near Caltaldo, and I see the spirit of an old man near Kellogg. The girl is wearing a white-colored dress with a high collar. She is petite. She had no expression on her face. She does not seem to see me. I wonder if it is the ghost of someone who was killed a long time ago in that area or on an old wagon trail or something? The man I see is also from another era, and it seems as though he is wearing some sort of animal skins on his back and shoulders, carries a long gun, has a leather hat and tall, worn out boots. He carries a worried, apprehensive look about him.*

Could the male entity be that of a man who, in 1883, buried his gold in the vicinity of Kellogg? The story, as told by the *Twin Falls Times* on December 9, 1913, tells of a man named Edward Cornelius and his partner, who traveled from Montana with a pack of gold on their donkeys. The men came through Prospect Creek Trail to Mullen Road and into Kellogg after hearing of the gold rush in the Silver Valley. They wanted to invest in as much real estate as their money could afford. When they arrived, they realized the rumors were exaggerated, and there was no big gold rush there. This meant that the land values were not going to be as prosperous as they had imagined. Frustrated, they decided to hide their gold for safety reasons while they decided what their next move was going to be. The men chose a "flat spot of land from the Kellogg Depot to the Bunker Hill and Sullivan Mills area." They packed their gold nuggets in a Dutch oven they had with them and buried the pot in the land right in the middle of a triangle of trees. Their markers? One fir tree and two pine trees. Then they went about their business. Unfortunately, before the men could return to retrieve their fortune, a fire had swept the area, burning down all the trees.

Cornelius supposedly searched for their gold for thirty long years, never to find it. Today, the gold would be worth a whopping $2,209,536.36. No wonder his restless spirit is still searching for his lost treasure.

It is said that there are a few more lost treasures in the Silver Valley. The famous bank and train robber Butch Cassidy (real name Robert LeRoy Parker, 1866–1908) and his gang supposedly buried some of their stolen loot somewhere between Spokane Falls and Wallace. That's a big distance to search for hidden money. The only clues are that it was buried north of the "old stagecoach road" and along a river next to a beaver dam. Since Cassidy reined terror for several decades, he and his gang could have acquired quite the sum of stolen money.

5

WALLACE

A Town Loaded with Ghosts

Every city is a ghost. New buildings rise upon the bones of the old so that each shiny steel beam, each tower of brick carries within it the memories of what has gone before, an architectural haunting. Sometimes you can catch a glimpse of these former incarnations in the awkward angle of a street or filigreed gate, an old oak door peeking out from a new facade, the plaque commemorating the spot that was once a battleground, which became a saloon and is now a park.
——Libba Bray

A ghost story from Annette:

> *I just bought a new house, and although I do not know if it is haunted, I know my dog Wheezle thinks it is. Sometimes when are watching TV late at night, Wheezy and I get an eerie feeling, and he goes over to the stairs and looks up toward my loft. He stares right at the two unfinished areas up there like he is seeing something. Sometimes I hear a loud bang and then he starts to bark. He refuses to go up the stairs. Sometimes when the clanking and banging gets really bad, Wheezle stares up there and his eyes go back and forth like he is watching something move around. It is scary. I have put four-leaf clovers on each of the posts on the stairs in hopes it can protect us.*

Of all the small towns in the Silver Valley, Wallace is by far the most haunted and is located forty-eight miles east of Coeur d'Alene. Almost every building

The creepy remains of abandoned buildings in the ghost town of Burke are sure to house a ghost or two. *Courtesy of author.*

has a spirit or two, although not all proprietors wanted to announce their presence. The small, century-old town has seen more than its share of tragedies, victories, murders, celebrities, outlaws and even a visit from President Theodore Roosevelt (1858–1919) in 1903. The film *Dante's Peak*, starring Pierce Brosnan and Linda Hamilton, was filmed in Wallace, with many of the locals appearing as extras. The films *Heaven's Gate* and *Tornado* were also filmed in Wallace.

The legendary movie star and pinup model Lana Turner (1921–1995) was born in Wallace, and some locals would like to think that the actress returned to Wallace after her death and that her ghost now graces the streets with her beauty. Her childhood home on Bank Street still exists, although vacant, its porch balcony and weathered front door are silent reminders of yesteryear. Lana was born at the Providence Hospital in Wallace and after a few years living in Burke Canyon, the family moved to Wallace in 1925. She then moved to Hollywood when she was a young girl, and during her long career, she became one of the highest paid women in the film business, with her contracts totaling over $50 million. After several bad marriages and some career ups and downs, Lana began dating mobster Johnny Stompanato, who reportedly had a violent temper. Their stormy relationship finally came to a screeching halt on April 4, 1958, in Lana's Beverly Hills home, when Stompanato was stabbed by Lana's daughter, Cheryl. After hours of listening to the two argue and Stompanato spewing threats of murdering all of them, the teenaged Cheryl grabbed a kitchen knife and stabbed Stompanato in the stomach, killing him. The case was considered one of self-defense. The paparazzi couldn't get enough of the drama, but things eventually calmed down. After all of that misfortune and Hollywood chaos, it is no wonder Lana's spirit may have returned to the peaceful and quiet life of the small town of Wallace.

Founded in 1884, the town was named after Colonel William Ross Wallace (1834–1901), a local farmer, who purchased eighty acres and built a small cabin on it. He soon played a key role in developing the mining in the entire region. He had mining interests in many places, including Idaho, California, Texas, New Mexico and Arizona. That was the beginning of what is now known as the "Center of the Universe." The town survived many horrific fires and floods, devastating almost the entire town over and over again. But the townspeople were determined to continue to rebuild their town, and by 1887, the first school was opened, along with multiple saloons, apartments, a hall and several shops. The town continued to grow and even included the addition of a few brothels. Some of the old buildings are reported to be haunted today. No one knows if the spirits are those of former patrons, madams or proprietors of Wallace, but one thing is certain: the town is full of ghosts.

JAMESON HOTEL

Maggie Still Waits

A ghost story from Keyra, former employee of Jameson Hotel in Wallace:

I work as a housekeeper at the Historic Jameson Saloon. I have had some outlandish things happen to me that can't truly be explained away. First, I would like to note I am currently the only housekeeper, so no one goes upstairs besides me when I am at work. One evening I was giving a couple a tour of the facility, so we walked upstairs, and I noticed the basketball that I left out for the little boy spirit to played with was gone. Upon stepping around two corners, I saw that ball in the middle of the hallway in front of room 6. I know some people will say that the ball was rolled down the hallway, but that explanation doesn't make sense. For the ball to be in the location it was, the ball would have to round two corners and in the dead middle of the hall. I put the ball back, and it has not been moved since then. Also, the doorknob to the Inn Keeper's was removed. So, I asked my boss if he had taken it, which he told me he didn't. Together, him and I searched the whole place, but we could not find it. It still has not been found, and it has been three months.

Wallace Junior/Senior High School had their homecoming at the Jameson on the banquet floor, and a female student reported seeing a woman.

The student was in the bathroom washing her hands when she looked up at the mirror and saw a woman standing behind her. So, she looked behind her and saw no one. Quickly, she dried her hands and left the bathroom. She saw the woman again as she was walking up the stairs to return to the banquet floor, but the woman was heading up the stairs. The student did not see the woman again for the rest of the evening. Through some research, she discovered the woman was Maggie, a spirit said to haunt the Jameson, waiting for her true love to come back to her and marry her like he promised so many years ago. In addition to these stories, employees have been grabbed on the shoulder, their hair pulled, hearing footsteps above the restaurant/bar and things being moved from their original spot. The group that came out was called Northwestern Paranormal Group and the Spokane Ghost Crew. We also just had a group of lawyers come in, and they stated that they heard footsteps, had knocking at their door and no one was there when they opened it. Also, room 4's door was locked when the patrons returned, and their key was inside, also they left their door opened when their group left.

The lovely, yet very haunted, Theodore Jameson's Steak and Billiards Hall was built in 1907 by Theodore F. Jameson (1843–1923) at 304 Sixth Street in Wallace. It replaced a wooden structure that had burned to the ground, like many other buildings, during the horrible fire in 1890. Jameson was born in Paris, Kentucky, and then moved to Missouri as a teenager. In 1870, he moved to San Francisco, then to Nevada, followed by South Dakota and then eventually made his way to Idaho around 1881. In 1884, Jameson opened a saloon in Eagle City near Murray, Idaho. He finally made his way to Wallace in 1889, where he built and opened the glorious and ornate Jameson Hotel that still exists today. The 1900 federal census lists him as a liquor merchant living at 270 High Street, and a few years later, he was known to live at his hotel on Sixth, which was recorded at a value of $18,280. Jameson was a member of the Wallace Lodges no. 54 and no. 331, F.O.E. Lodge and the Elks Lodge.

In the 1920s, the place was operated as a bar and restaurant, with several hotel rooms for rent upstairs. At that time, a beautiful woman named Maggie, who was in her early twenties, would travel by train to Wallace from St. Louis, Missouri, where she waited for her lover to meet up with her, so they could get married and start a life together. The legend goes that she would spend weeks at the Jameson waiting for her lover. Sometimes those weeks would turn to months. This desperate scenario went on for a number of years. Maggie, a friendly gal, eventually became known in town by the locals. Then one year, she left Wallace and never returned. Did she finally give up on her lover's false promise of returning to get her? Did she meet someone else and fall in love? Rumors persisted that a more tragic fate happened that halted their dreams—that her lover had died in St. Louis due to some catastrophe that involved a train. Some believe that Maggie eventually died of a broken heart waiting for him.

Other legends tell of a young Wallace girl who went with a group of friends to a football game, where she was killed. The story changes once again and tells of a young girl named Maggie who was almost a gypsy, traveling back and forth between St. Louis and Wallace. Maggie would help out at the Jameson, cleaning, cooking and checking in the guests. Her room overlooked the city's sidewalks, where Maggie would spend hours looking out the window. Possibly, she was daydreaming of her future plans. Maggie supposedly died during one of the train trips, and her spirit returned to the one place she always felt at home—the Jameson.

Several spirits haunt the Jameson Hotel in Wallace. Strangely, many EVPs are recorded in a bathroom of the hotel. *Courtesy of author.*

Strange happenings started to occur at the Jameson Hotel. Was it really Maggie's spirit returning to her favorite place, where she felt welcomed and safe, that was creating the odd occurrences, or was it mere coincidence? Employees reported seeing apparitions of a female host in the halls and bedrooms. Icy cold chills would sweep through the rooms, and in Maggie's former suite, the impression of a head on a pillow was seen by housekeepers, even when the room had been vacant.

In 1979, the hotel's saloon, dining room and six guest rooms were renovated. Renovations are popularly known to stir up spiritual encounters. To this day, the spirit of Maggie is said to haunt the Jameson and sometimes her sister building, the Sweets.

A story from Shaffer, former manager of the Jameson in the early 1990s, as told to locals:

The bedroom where the ghost of Maggie is said to haunt the Jameson Hotel in Wallace. *Courtesy of author.*

One night around 2:00 a.m., Shaffer said he was sleeping alone in the dark, quiet hotel when his dog suddenly and uncharacteristically started barking and growling. Shaffer had been waiting for some late-arriving guests to appear, though they never did. "The dog was going crazy," he said.

A fan had been turned on in his suite, and the door, which he had closed, had been opened. Awakened by the dog's terror, he soon heard light footsteps just outside his room. "There was somebody in the hallway," he said. He grabbed a robe and dashed downstairs to check the front door. No one was there. The place was still locked and empty. Another time, when the hotel was temporarily closed during an off-season, Shaffer had been there alone checking the inventory in the cramped basement.

"And there is like a party going on, all of the sudden, upstairs," he said. "Toilets are flushing, there's people walking around, there's noise going on." Alarmed, Shaffer rushed upstairs to investigate.

"Totally locked up and nobody is here," he said, recalling what he found. Back in the late 1970s or early 1980s, some paranormal investigators from England came to do an investigation at the hotel. They quickly concluded there was a second ghost, too, a man named Ollie. "He was kind of putting the moves on Maggie," Shaffer said.

The Jameson Hotel is full of ghosts. A male spirit named Ollie tends to touch women as they move about the rooms. *Courtesy of author.*

Some passersby claim to see of the apparition Maggie peering out through the window downstairs where the piano sits. Some people claim they have heard the faint sound of piano music at night. Curious ghost hunters consistently investigate the Jameson in search of proof of ghosts using spirit boxes, EVP recorders and EMF meters. It is hard to tell whose spirit (or spirits) is haunting the building, as countless people have lodged in the rooms since its beginning in 1907. As suggested, a ghost does not necessarily have to die in the building to haunt it. Many times, spirits simply refuse to leave because they love the building or town so much.

A ghost story from the author:

I was at the Jameson Hotel with Mark Porter from Spokane Paranormal Society. When we were downstairs, we got many "words" on his voice box. When we moved to the next floor, Mark and I sat down in Maggie's room. No words at all came through. After a bit, we gathered our things to move to another area of the hotel. As I got up, I felt as if someone had wrapped their arms around me from behind, like a bear hug. The hairs on my forearms were all standing up where I felt "hands" on me. Mark said, "What's

*happening?" So, I told him. He said that another presence, a male entity
named Ollie, was known to "touch" women. I quickly left the room, asking
Ollie to please not touch me.*

People who have stayed in Wallace during the 1920s included a Maggie
Angus, who would have been twenty-one years old in 1920. She was logged as
staying at Ward 3 at the Providence Hospital later in Wallace. Could an illness
explain why Maggie disappeared, never again to stay at her favorite hotel while
living? Does her spirit still roam the Jameson waiting for her lover to return, only
to eventually die from a broken heart? Did she really return to her hometown
back East? No one will ever truly know the final whereabouts of the mysterious
Maggie, who actively haunts both the Jameson and Sweets Hotels.

SWEETS HOTEL

Who Is Haunting It?

The Sweets Hotel is connected to the Jameson Saloon, and even thought
the upstairs is vacant and in need of restoration, locals feel the ghost of
Maggie or some other spirit roaming the cold hallways and empty rooms.
Could the ghost be that of the original proprietor, Lewis L. Sweet (1857–
1929), who does not want to leave his beloved hotel? Sweet came to Idaho
from Pennsylvania. He was known to be a very gentle and caring man. He
worked in the lumber business at the early age of eighteen, and then in 1881,
he came to work in the Salmon River mines. Later, he moved to Portland,
Oregon, and became involved in the meat business. In 1891, he returned to
Wallace with only a horse and cart and two dimes. A man of means, and an
opportunist, over the years, he opened a saloon in Gem with a partner by
the name of Wm. R. Stimson, ran the Bimetallic Hotel & Bar in Wallace,
operated a confection and cigar store in Gem and finally found his home in
1901, when he began running the Wallace Hotel.

He was active in the local festivals and parades, was a member of the
Eagles, was married to a woman named Emma and he dabbled in certificates.
Several mining companies held their annual meetings at the Sweets. Sweet
ran the Wallace Hotel on Sixth and Cedar in the early 1900s, which proudly
advertised the selling of Budweiser beer on draught and Turkish baths.
Although local sheriff Angus Sutherland tried to put a stop to gambling in
Wallace, in 1906, Sweet was a participant in a $6,000, three-day poker game

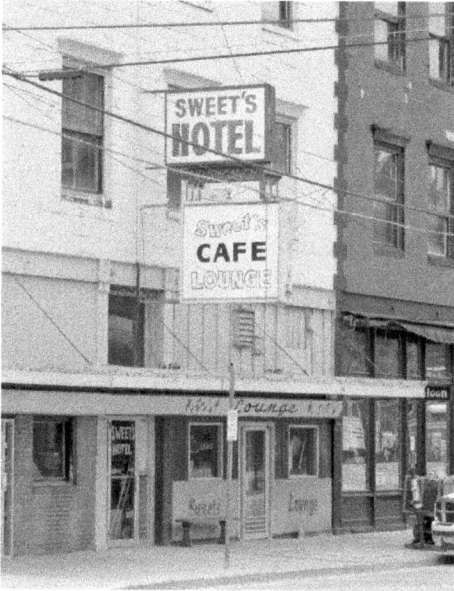

Sweets Hotel, located to the left of Jameson Hotel in Wallace, is also haunted. Is it Maggie or another spirit? *Courtesy of author.*

that started at the Wallace Hotel and finished at the Ryan Hotel across the street. Sweet came out the big winner and was $2,000 richer than he was on Friday.

A bond salesman named M.B. Rice from Spokane came to Wallace for business during the Thanksgiving holiday in 1906, stayed at the Wallace Hotel for several days, never checked out and disappeared from the face of Earth. He was never heard from again, and his body was never found. Was he a victim of foul play? No more articles or information can be located about the fate of Mr. Rice. Could this be the ghost that haunts the Sweets? Or is it the ghost of Mr. Lewis Sweet himself who roams the halls of the old hotel he loved so much while alive? Sweet had many friends in Wallace and was known as an upstanding and well-liked citizen. The mystery of *who* is actually haunting the Sweets remains just that—a mystery.

RYAN HOTEL

Miss Montgomery Helps Out

The beautiful, brick Ryan Hotel on Cedar Street in Wallace is haunted by multiple ghosts—all friendly and happy to still reside there long after their departures. Mediums who have visited the Ryan tell the owners that these entities *choose* to be there because they love it so much. Some spirits are there all the time, such as Miss Montgomery, and others tend to "come and go."

Frank Ryan (1859–?), ran the beautiful Ryan Hotel located at 608 Cedar Street in Wallace. Ryan was born in New York to Irish parents. Not much is known about him, but records show that he married Anne

Gearon in 1894. The 1900 census has him working at a hotel at age forty and living at 264 Sixth Street in Wallace. In 1910, he was working as a lead miner, and in 1920, he was living on High Street in town and working as a hotel clerk.

Built in 1903, the Ryan Hotel has seen many changes in the little town of Wallace. It served as a residential hotel to local miners, and some of the rooms were occupied by long-term tenants. It is one of the few buildings that survived the horrendous fire in 1910 that destroyed most of the town. The Ryan still stands through the test of time. Inside, the historic details remain intact, and the beautiful lobby desk at the top of the stairs transports guests back in time. The original residential mail slots are still used as registration card holders. The rooms host many original features and antique furniture, as well as hand-painted glass light fixtures and lovely wood built in medicine cabinets. There was an extensive renovation in about 1933, which currently reflects that time period. Always meticulously clean and tidy, it's no wonder the ghosts don't want to leave.

Room 11 was occupied by Miss Dorothy Montgomery (1907–1998) for about forty-three years and is the liveliest for paranormal activity. She was

The historic Ryan Hotel in Wallace is haunted by several friendly ghosts. *Courtesy of author.*

The haunted room in the Ryan Hotel, where the ghost of Miss Montgomery resides. *Courtesy of Donna, owner of Ryan Hotel.*

a local third grade teacher, who loved the Ryan Hotel and her room so much that she has continued to be an active and consistent presence at the hotel. Her space is lovingly decorated with vintage school charm that surely makes her spirit feel right at home. Dorothy is a stern, protective and helpful presence at the Ryan. She reportedly offers "nudges" for the owner Donna and other team members to assist in the everyday operations of the hotel.

A story shared by Donna:

> *Miss Montgomery is a very special entity at the Ryan Hotel. I often get little nudges from her in the right direction, changing my course and going against my normal routine. Many times, if a guest accidentally leaves something important in their room, I will get a strong feeling to go to that room, even if I am on my way to another task. Once, a woman left her laptop on the bed, and I was making my way to another room when I got a strong feeling to go back and check that particular room. Sure enough, there was her laptop, and I was able to call the guest immediately and let her know to come back and get it. This saved her the hassle of mailing an item or a trip back to Wallace to retrieve it.*

As a teacher, Miss Montgomery was known to have an extreme attention to detail, be very organized. No doubt that at the Ryan, she kept her room clean and orderly the whole time she lived here. Once, when I had finished cleaning her room and thought it was ready for the next guest, she gave me a little prompting to check the left side of the bed. As I am meticulous about making the rooms as perfect and clean as possible at all times, I thought, "The bed looks great, why recheck it?" But sure enough, Miss Montgomery had noticed that the linen underneath the bedspread had a little ruffle in it—something both of us would not have liked. I smiled, smoothed out the linen and thanked her for her attention to detail. Another time, an item was moved in her room, and I know it was because she would have disagreed with it being there. It made me wonder, do ghosts have feelings, too? I had never thought about that possibility before.

The Ryan is home to several other ghosts as well. A male entity is known to hang out in one of the rooms. A guest once saw what appeared to be a pilot from another era walking down the hall and into another room, when a ghost radar device was recently put in that room, the word FLIGHT appeared on the screen.

Dorothy Montgomery (*middle, white sweater*) protects her beloved Ryan Hotel, where she lived for over forty years. *Courtesy of Donna, owner of Ryan Hotel, picture supplied by Amy Lynn, Wallace resident.*

Several male spirits come and go at the Ryan. They could be any of many men who held offices or enjoyed staying at the Ryan in the early 1900s. Could the ghost be that of proprietor P.F. Geardon in 1909? Does he still think he is managing it? Or could the male entity be the man who was in charge of the dining room (he was probably working out of another building in town) in 1908, Mr. W.A. McIntyre? In 1917, the oldest stock brokerage firm in the Coeur d'Alenes was in the Ryan building, with broker James F. Howarth keeping his office there. In 1921, the assistant treasurer of the Phoenix Mining & Milling Company, E.C. Allen, spent many of his days there. Do their spirits still roam the halls or sit at the desks in their favorite rooms?

Since the ghosts are noted to be friendly and choose to remain there, it could be because they still enjoy a good poker game or two. In 1906, the biggest stud poker game in the Coeur d'Alene region was partially held at the Ryan. The $6,000 game started at the Wallace Hotel on Friday and finished on Sunday at the Ryan. The *Elk City Mining News* reported on December 22, 1906, "The biggest winner was L.L. Sweet, proprietor of the Wallace Hotel, winning $2,000. Ben Skonnard was runner up with $1,600 take home." Perhaps the ghosts of the fun-filled men are still playing poker in one of the rooms at the Ryan.

A couple appears in one of the back rooms, playfully enjoying their "stay" at the Ryan. They seem to be passing through, as their spirits are not consistently present. Possibly these ghosts are that of a happy couple, James Watson and J. Poutcher, who were married at the Ryan in 1912.

Another ghost is that of a young girl, who actively bounces around one of the rooms, although thankfully not on the bed. Not much is known about this tender spirit, it is suggested that she is just very energetic and happy. The owner of the Ryan for almost eight years, Donna, has been told that there are four ghosts residing there all the time. Several other spirits tend to be more sporadic. One thing is certain: many future ghosts might end up staying at the Ryan Hotel, too, as it is one of the warmest and most welcoming hotels in Wallace.

THE BROOKS HOTEL

A Haunted Former Hospital

A ghost story from Gary Stanley:

Several years ago, we had a guest who said she had seen an apparition upstairs. So, we went upstairs, and she took some pictures and a video with her phone. She did a complete circle as she did this. When we looked back on the photos and video, we all saw the partial figure of a woman wearing a gown looking right at the camera. You could see a lady's face. As we were in the old operating room—this was originally built as a hospital—the gown would make sense. The operating room had a marble floor with a skylight for the surgeons. There was a morgue in the basement.

A ghost story from Rachel of the Brooks Hotel:

We hear footsteps a lot when we are cleaning the rooms—sometimes when I know for a fact that we are the only people there. Many of us have heard the phantom footsteps, but we never feel anything scary or creepy. We would like to think it is just one of the former guests from years gone by who loves the Brooks and just doesn't want to leave.

The Brooks Hotel, located at 500 Cedar Street in Wallace, was named after Samuel Brooks. It was originally built as part of the local hospital, complete with a morgue in the basement and an operating room upstairs. This only adds to the mystery of who the ghosts are that roam the Brooks. Could it be a former patient? That original building, built in 1905, was partially destroyed by a fire. It was later rebuilt.

The building has been many other things other than a hotel. Besides being a former hospital, it was Morrow's Department Store, Baker Dry Goods and was once called the Day Building. When the Day brothers purchased the building in 1916, they added another twenty-five feet to the building, and a seam can be seen where this addition was completed. This addition was for their mining operations and was designed by Spokane architect Albert Held. The men had their offices upstairs. With so many wonderful people being part of the Brooks over the last century-plus, the ghosts could be any of them still walking the halls of the building.

PROVIDENCE HOSPITAL

Miracle of the Coeur d`Alenes

Haunted places and ghost stories don't always have to be scary—sometimes they are uplifting and spiritual. Much like the Cataldo Mission church is known to emit a loving and euphoric feeling, the story of Providence Hospital, erected in Wallace in 1891 and saved from flames, is a wonderful and endearing story. The legend goes that the superior of the hospital, Sister Anthony of Jesus, Sp., heard of the fire in Wallace on August 20, 1910, at 9:00 p.m. and was so desperate to save the hospital that she immediately fell to her knees and fervently prayed for it to be spared from the flames. In return, she promised to erect a statue of Jesus of the Sacred Heart in front of the infirmary.

Sister Joseph of Antioch, Sp, just twenty-one years old at the time, had bravely left the safety of the last coach out of town to return to the needs of the three invalids lying in the basement of the hospital in Wallace, awaiting certain death. As she watched the fire come closer and closer, she eventually sat on the steps and prayed and wept, waiting to die a tragic death at such a young age.

And her prayers were answered at that very moment. At 9:00 p.m., the wind changed direction, and the burning flames mysteriously and quickly moved away from the hospital. Just minutes before, the flames were so close that it was reported the paint was blistering on the other side of the building. Was the hospital saved by a guardian angel watching over the Sisters of Providence in their time of need or by Jesus himself? It was truly a miracle.

The tragic 1910 fire that burned over three million acres and spread through Washington, Idaho and Montana had left two-thirds of Wallace destroyed. Countless homes and buildings were burned to the ground, leaving almost three hundred people homeless. Many livestock and wildlife lost their lives too. In Wallace, several people were blinded by the smoke, and forty private homes were reduced to ashes. The area from Seventh Street to Canton Street was completely burned to the ground. The only buildings left on the east end of Wallace were Providence Hospital and the nearby Federal Land Company mills.

It was estimated that almost one hundred Wallace businesses were destroyed and had sustained huge losses, including the Coeur d'Alene Hardware Company warehouse ($150,000), the Brewery ($80,000), Pacific Hotel ($60,000), Coeur d'Alene Iron Works ($80,000), Oregon Railway &

The Providence Hospital in Wallace was saved from destruction by divine intervention in 1909. *Courtesy of University of Idaho, Courtesy of PG 8, Item X182b, Barnard-Stockbridge Collection, University of Idaho Library Special Collections and Archives, Moscow, Idaho. Public domain.*

Navigation depot ($60,000), Times Printing Company ($25,000) and the Worstell Furniture Company ($50,000).

Later, as promised, the statue of Jesus was erected in front of the hospital. When the hospital was closed in 1968 and later torn down, the statue was donated to a local museum.

The horrifying personal account of the fire was later told by Sister Joseph of Antioch, courtesy of Providence Archives, Seattle, Washington:

> *J.M.J., To comply to your request I shall try to relate as correctly as possible the details of the Wallace fire on August 20th, 1910. On April 15th, 1910, I came to Wallace, Idaho as my first missionary post. The first few months of my religious life were spent in peaceful, quiet atmosphere and I was very happy to devote myself to the care of the poor and infirm, but a big trial was in store for me which will soon bring sorrow to my peaceful life. The dear good God in His infinite goodness saw fit that I should share in His sufferings. During the summer of 1910, the weather*

An unidentified sister at Providence standing by the promised Sacred Heart of Jesus statue. *Courtesy of Providence Archives, Seattle.*

was very dry, we had no rain for weeks. Towards the end of July and beginning of August, the sky was dark and thick with smoke. We could feel the forest-fire coming nearer and nearer; there was a falling of ashes on the roofs and porches every morning for several weeks. But all those signs of near-by fires did not frighten the people of Wallace as they were under the impression that fire never works down-hills, therefore no precautions were taken to protect themselves.

On the evening of August 20th, about 8.00 o'clock, when the forest fire carried by a strong wind, reached the top of the mountains surrounding our city, it began to spread rapidly down the mountains—a real panic took place, in a very short time everybody had to leave town to save their lives. As the danger became greater and closer it was necessary to remove the patients from the hospital. To help us in our distress the Northern Pacific Railway employees managed to bring a caboose and a coach on the railroad track in front of the hospital.

In less than fifteen minutes Chaplain, Sisters, patients, employees and every-body else were aboard the train en route for Missoula. (All, except my poor self)—"like Moses who was in the dark in the cellar when the lights went out"—I had gone to the basement to try to save three old gentlemen patients, who didn't seem to realize the danger they were in. The County Physician tried to persuade them to go on the train with the others, but without success; so he left them as they preferred not to be disturbed. Not wishing them to burn, I tried again by signs to draw their attention to the fire, showed them the flames through the window, on the hills. My English was very limited at that time, and it was during that time of my hard experience that I learned the word "FIRE." I never forgot it and never will forget it either.

Not long after the fire broke out in the city, telegraph and all electric wires were burned which left the entire place in complete darkness except for the light caused be the flames. We had to use candles to find our way through the house. This train left Wallace at 8.30 p.m. and reached Missoula only at 8.00 am the next day. Ordinarily this trip is made in less than five hours.

The personnel of our house was received with great sympathy at Saint Patrick's Hospital. The Chaplain, Father Francis Bonora said Mass at the Hospital and the sisters had the consolation of hearing it and receive Holy Communion in thanks-giving for having been protected.

Shortly after the train had left Wallace they called everyone by name to see if all were there; they soon found out that I was missing. Some of the sisters wanted to get off the train to fetch me but the conductor refused as it was too dangerous, there was fire all along the way the train had to stop occasionally to wait for the fire to be extinguished on the track.

The Chaplain carried the Blessed Sacrament with him all the way and he had to sit in the coal bin with a few of the sisters.

When the sisters left Wallace there was no hope of saving the hospital; all doors were therefore left opened. If the three old gentlemen did not get excited while in the basement, about the fire, nevertheless shortly afterwards they all got out of the house and were glad to get in the big wagon with the rest of us.

You can Imagine how I felt when I came up from the basement to find everybody else gone. I thought, Well, I am all alone what am I going to do? I looked around and not a soul was to be found in the house. I went out on the front porch and sat there a while to look at the fire about one block or two from the house. Walking back and forth about the house I met a doctor who was much surprised to see me. He went at once to the engineer who was busy trying to save the horses and wagon, he told him about me. He hitched the horses and I got in the wagon with the three old patients, the orderly and the engineer for driver and we started, for where? We didn't know. Imagine my fear being on the road, the only woman, at 9:00 pm going out of town in a mad rush with two wild horses frightened by the raging fire. I asked the engineer, (who spoke very good French) where he was going to take us. "Where there is no fire" was the answer, adding that there was a French lady living somewhere in that direction, I will try to locate her. He asked of everyone we met on the way where Mrs. Lemieux lived. It was 10:00 pm when we found her place. We were received with open arms by this good lady and she was so happy to give me hospitality for the night. The next day she took me to Spokane, Washington. I was so happy to be with the Sisters of Providence once more, at Sacred Heart Hospital. On the way tears were rolling down on my cheeks, and the engineer noticed it, he said, "Ma soeur, ne pleurex pas, je vais prendre soin de vous." It was a little consolation in my great sorrow. That morning while yet at Mrs. Lemieux, during our breakfast, they told me they were going to take me to Spokane on the first train that would leave Wallace. I said, "I have no money." "We have some," said the good Mr. Lemieux.

Another incident worth mentioning; on the same evening of August 20th, Our Lady of Lourdes Academy, situated at the other end of town, was also surrounded by fire. The parish priest, Father Becker, told the sisters to take the Blessed Sacrament to the hospital, so Sister Mary Carmilita had the privilege to open the Tabernacle and remove the Sacred Hosts and carried them to the hospital.

Sister Anthony of Jesus, who was our superior at that time, was absent; she had gone to Missoula to greet our new Provincial, Mother Frederick, who was coming to take charge of the province. When our dear Sister Superior heard of this conflagration she promised to erect a statue of the Sacred Heart of Jesus in front of the hospital if the house was spared. At the same instant the wind changed direction and everything was left intact, not even a small hole could be found anywhere.

As a climax, some large oil-tanks exploded in the foundry situated at a short distance from the hospital; for some time then the hospital disappeared in a cloud of flames from this explosion. About 80 lives were lost in Wallace and surrounding vicinity in this fire, also 30 to 40 homes were destroyed.

These are all the details I can recall from this memorable day of my greatest trial in my missionary life."

—S.J. of A. (Sr. Joseph of Antioch)

The great fire of 1910 was noted as one of the worst fires in history. Over 1,700 fires blazed and destroyed three million acres of timber. The fire went from August 20 until August 21, and the smoke could be seen as far east as New York. The total death toll is unknown, as an unfortunate number of people died even after the fire, due to the smoke damage in their lungs.

PULASKI TRAIL

A Hero Still Protects

Some say the spirit of Edward Crocket Pulaski (1866–1931) still roams the town of Wallace, and particularly the area in the woods where he almost lost his life, along with almost fifty other men. Pulaski became a United States forest ranger in 1908. Just two years later, he was running for his life—literally. As the red glowing flames terrorized the small town, Pulaski and his crew were at an area known as Placer Creek, ten miles southwest of Wallace. Nearby, firefighters were dying. At Big Creek, twelve men died and three were blinded. The fifty-man crew, led by Ranger John Bell, was forced to lie face down in the water, as flames burned their backs and necks. At Pine Creek, three died and five were blinded. At Setzer Creek, twenty-eight men died. All around the area, men were being burned alive or dying from smoke inhalation, and unfortunately, many were buried where they had died, never receiving a proper funeral or the honor they deserved.

The Palouse winds were recorded to hit seventy-five miles per hour at times, and ash and smoke from the burn was carried over two thousand feet into the air. People's lungs burned hot, and many were permanently damaged.

Pulaski, in his early forties, was manning a crew of about fifty men during the fire at Placer Creek on August 20, 1910. Fearing the worst, he knew his men were no match for the flames. He said, "Men, it's no use, we got to try to make it to Wallace, that's our only chance."

He quickly led his men into an old mining opening, named the Nicholson Tunnel, where they covered the entrance with water-drenched blankets, hoping to survive the fire. Pulaski, wielding his pistol, threatened to shoot any man who tried to leave the safety of the tunnel. He ordered his men to lie face down in the mud. Pulaski's hands became blistered from the heat, and soon, all of the men were unconscious. In the middle of the night, one man escaped the tunnel and made his way to Wallace, giving the grave news that all the men had died in the confines of the tunnel.

But he was wrong. As search-and-rescue men made their way back to the Nicholson Tunnel, they found only five men and two horses dead. Pulaski, their brave hero, was lying in the mud.

One man cried out, "The boss is dead!" Much to their surprise, Pulaski slowly lifted his head and exclaimed, "Like hell he is," although he was temporarily blind. Stories report that Pulaski's wife, having been told her beloved husband was dead, was found roaming the streets of Wallace, inconsolable. She must have beamed like a lighthouse when, surprisingly, her loving husband was seen staggering toward the town in bad shape but alive.

Rain finally blessed the area on the August 23, halting one of the worse fires in history. After all was said and done, the Big Burn had consumed over three million acres and run hot for thirty-six hours. It was recorded that over eighty people were killed—seventy-eight of whom were firefighters. In Montana the towns of Taft, DeBorgia, Henderson, Tuscor and Haugan were all destroyed. In Idaho, Falcon and Grand Forks were in ashes, along with most of Wallace. The wild spaces burned were the Bitterroot areas, along with the Cabinet, Clearwater, Coeur d'Alene, Flathead, Kaniksu, Kootenai, Lewis and Clark, Lolo and St. Joe national forests. Thousands of fish were dead in all of the streams.

Many policies about firefighting were changed after the Big Burn, and a new type of axe was invented by and named after Pulaski himself. A hiking trail outside of Wallace is designated in honor of Pulaski, and in 1921, a 1910 fire memorial was located at the Nine Mile Cemetery in town. Today, while driving I-90 south from Wallace to St. Regis in Montana, a forty-five-mile trek, one can experience the vast expanse of the old burn zone.

Ghost hunters relay stories of glowing orbs, strange noises, apparitions and more at the Nine Mile Cemetery. Could these be the spirits of the men who lost their lives in the fire? Or other ghosts who haunt the cemetery for unknown reasons? Some claim to have seen the apparition of a man walking near the tunnel on the Pulaski Trail. Who could that ghost be? One of the firefighters who died or some other citizen who was killed by the flames? It is uncertain who the spirit is, but the ghost could be one of many victims from that horrible tragedy.

SIXTH STREET MELODRAMA THEATER
More Than Just Shows

It's a big spooky place when you're in it alone. It's like you can hear all the whispers of all the voices of all the actors who ever played here. Kind of creepy. Like a church can be creepy when it's empty. You ever been in a church after hours?

—*Benjamin R. Smith*

The Sixth Street Melodrama Theater in Wallace is said to be haunted, and many paranormal investigators try to communicate with the spirits who reside there. Spirit boxes retrieve words from the ghosts that signify a life from the past—one of bordellos and even a madam. During an investigation, the words *money*, *leave*, *angry* and *silence* came through. Could this be the spirit of a former madam from long ago? Are her lips sealed about the patrons who visited the brothel as they were in the years when she ran her business? Objects mysteriously move without cause and faint whispers can be heard in the building, but no one truly knows who the spirit (or spirits) is that lingers inside. Old theaters are also commonly haunted by former actors and actresses who simply cannot give up their glory days on the stage. That brings a whole new meaning to the phrase, "The show must go on."

The Melodrama is the oldest-standing wooden structure in Wallace's Historic District. At one time, it housed Frank's Paint & Wallpaper store, with the Luxette Bordello running upstairs. The Luxette was run by a kind and considerate woman named Delores Arnold. As beautiful as a movie star, the madam was liked in town and often supported community events. She was said to donate money to the local schools and drove a 1958 Cadillac, with her poodle riding shotgun. She later moved her business to the Arment Building (above the Silver Corner), and her former building became a costume and prop storage for the theater.

The red-light district shut down in the late 1980s, and Delores was rumored to have moved to Reno. She eventually suffered from Alzheimer's disease.

The Sixth Street Melodrama, once a brothel, is a hot spot for paranormal activity and offers great theater performances. *Courtesy of author.*

NINE MILE CEMETERY
A Murderer Haunts from the Grave

A ghost story from Sarah Reasor McPherson of Silver Lining Paranormal:

> *My son, daughter-in-law and myself went up to investigate the Nine Mile Cemetery. Was pretty quiet until I seen three flashing lights. The equipment we were using started going crazy, and we started getting responses to our questions. When asked, "What is your name?" it responded with "Mia." We looked all over for a grave with that name and found nothing. Then on the spirit box we began getting some creepy noises and the word "evil." I immediately said we only welcome good spirits and a very evil laugh came over the spirit box. We left.*

Many locals and tourists claim to see strange lights and orbs at the old cemetery just outside of Wallace, and they even capture whispers and voices on tape recorders. These could be from any number of spirits, as the grave marker dates go back to the 1880s. Originally, the cemetery was three separate areas: the United, the Miners Union and the Catholic. Now, they are just divided into three sections. All walks of life are buried at Nine Mile Cemetery. The influenza epidemic that ran through the Silver Valley claimed almost seventy lives in 1918 and 1919, mostly men in their mid-thirties. The famous local hero and firefighter Ed Pulaski is buried there, as well as the well-loved Wallace legend and businessman Harry Magnuson (1895–1986). Prize fighter Guido Bardelli, also known as the Battling Bull of Burke (1907–1984), is also buried there.

But it is likely the hauntings are part of a well-known murder scandal that included an old town mayor, Herman Rossi Sr. (1870–1937), and his wife, Mabel. Herman shot and killed her lover, a local musician named Clarence "Gabe" Dahlquist (1889–1916), in the lobby of the Samuels Hotel in the town of Wallace. Perhaps he is still contemplating his actions from the grave, over one hundred years after the tragic murder. Dahlquist's twenty-seven-year-old body got shipped back to Omaha, Nebraska. The story began to unfold on the evening of June 30, 1916. Rossi had been out of town on business, when he discovered that his wife had been enjoying the company of Dahlquist while he was gone. Rossi had gone to Boise to participate in the Republican Party's platform deliberations.

The furious Rossi marched to the Samuel's Hotel on the corner of Cedar and Seventh, wielding a .38-caliber revolver. Dahlquist was seated in the lobby with friends when Rossi approached him. Rossi hit the man on the head with his gun several times. Dahlquist proceeded to fight him off and started to run away but didn't get very far. Rossi raised his hand and fired a shot at Dahlquist. The bullet raged through one of the man's lungs. Rossi was going to shoot the man a second time, but he was urged by the hotel clerks, George Baxter and Mrs. Laura Stone, to stop. Later, Baxter testified from the stand that he implored Rossi, "For God's sake, Herman, don't shoot!" Stone testified that she begged Rossi to not do something "he would always regret." Rossi relented but not before threatening that Dahlquist better leave town immediately or else.

After the shooting, Rossi made his way back to the street, where two of his friends, Julius Goodrich and Walter Hanson, ran into him when Rossi mumbled that he had encountered trouble at the Samuels. The men parted from Rossi and soon learned of the shooting at the hotel. The men immediately went over to Rossi's office, where they told Rossi that he had actually shot Dahlquist. To this Rossi stated, "If I shot him I didn't know it, and I am sorry." Later, Rossi gave himself up to the police but was released that same night. The injured Dahlquist was sent to Providence Hospital in Wallace but died the next day.

Mabel was known as a drinker, and this may have had a big part in the scenario. Rossi was a pillar in the community and a former mayor. It was known that Rossi was of great importance in real estate dealings in the Coeur d'Alene region and as a strong businessman. At Mabel's press conference, Mrs. Rossi told her Spokane lawyer that her husband was physically abusive to her during their marriage. Mabel was reported as stating in the *Tacoma Times* on November 19, "When the matter is all over I think the public will not believe that Mr. Rossi is the angel without wings and that I am the vile creature that he and his so-called friends would have the public believe me to be."

In the *Evening Capital News*, the image of Mr. Rossi is exposed differently. He claimed to have spent a small fortune on new furnishings for their home to try to make Mabel happy. More money (reportedly $600 to $1,000 per month) was spent on rehab to try to get Mabel to quit drinking. It was known that Rossi proudly took Mabel on his business travels to New York and Washington, where she basically behaved herself. But it was recorded that two years before the murder, after a bad drinking spree in Coeur d'Alene, Mabel had plans of separation and possibly divorce—definite trouble in paradise. Their marriage remained on rocky ground until the murder of her close friend, Dahlquist. Mabel denied any relations between Clarence and herself.

But Rossi was freed of the murder charge and acquitted on October 14. The jury debated for less than an hour before returning with a decision of not guilty. Rossi's attorney had originally pleaded his case, employing a temporary insanity defense. (Although two state physicians testified that Rossi *was* sane at the time of the murder.) He filed for divorce soon after, which Mabel contested. The Rossi battle continued. After the divorce was finalized, Rossi remarried Bernyce Ewing a year later.

The funeral procession for Dahlquist was held in Wallace and was one of the most well-attended events in town. This left many questioning, should Rossi have gotten off on the murder charges? Dahlquist was definitely liked in the community; perhaps the ruling should have been different. Although Dalquist was liked in Wallace, when Rossi's not guilty verdict was announced, it was greeted by the community with celebration and relief. Mabel reportedly fled to California and was never seen again in Wallace.

Who is haunting this old and beautiful cemetery? It is hard to tell. Until the spirits of Nine Mile Cemetery unveil their true identities, the mystery of the paranormal activity remains unsolved.

BURKE

Almost a Ghost Town

A ghost story from Sandy in Wallace:

> *I love to explore ghost towns, so when I heard about Burke, I could not wait to go see it. Unfortunately, the remaining buildings are all blocked off now by chain link fence, probably because of safety or possibly people had been vandalizing it. Sad. Anyway, I was taking pictures with my new camera, and I could have sworn I saw a face peering out from one of the windows of the old buildings. I zoomed in as fast as I could but did not see it again. Possibly, it was a trick of the light, but I could have sworn I saw a man's face, dirty, like it was covered in smoke or dirt. I wondered if it was the ghost of one of the miners from long ago.*

Although a small scattering of residents still live there, one of the best ghost towns in the Silver Valley is a little town called Burke (originally called Bayard), just a few miles from Wallace, Idaho. The town derived its name

Abandoned homes in the ghost town of Burke are both beautiful and eerie. *Courtesy of author.*

This old postcard of the Tiger Inn at Burke shows the one-of-a-kind hotel that had a railroad track and a river running through it. *Courtesy of Wikipedia public domain.*

The area of northern Idaho was so popular that even Wyatt Earp and his brothers opened a saloon in the town of Eagle City. *Drawing courtesy of the Columbus Journal, January 27, 1897.*

from a prominent man named John Muse Burke (1849–1908), who was well known throughout the West, and who took a great interest in the Tiger Mine.

Ghost towns are a mirror into the past and can be both eerie and fascinating. As land is getting more valuable, ghost towns are becoming scarcer. In the little town of Burke, Idaho, the creepy remains of mining buildings and tunnels offer a glimpse into the area's profitable yet troubled past. Where there's silver, there's money; where there's money, there's sometimes trouble. Burke and its nearby towns are no exception to that rule. Some claim they see flickering lights from inside old, abandoned buildings—the residual sounds of mining coming from inside abandoned mines and faces from long ago peering out broken windows. Could these be spirits from the past or simply overactive imaginations running wild?

The start of Burke's flourish was during the silver and lead mining boom in 1884. Hundreds of men rushed to the Coeur d'Alene region in search of riches, including the famous Wyatt Earp and his brothers, who ran a tent saloon in nearby Eagle City. Of the four Earp brothers, it was noted that Virgil was the oldest, Wyatt the wisest, Warren the foolhardiest and Julian the bravest. Some documents suggest that another famous name Calamity Jane enjoyed visiting the cluster of small towns cradled between the steep and rocky canyons.

Two trains, the Northern Pacific and the Oregon Railroad Company, moved ore from Burke to nearby Wallace. The town itself was squeezed in between two hills, and the area was a mere three hundred feet wide. When the railroad moved to Burke in 1887, it was said that businesses on the main street had to roll back their awnings each time the trains came through, or else the trains would tear them clean off the buildings as they roared past. Locals disagree with this theory and state that the awnings were simply rolled up so they would not get singed by burning cinders shooting from the tracks.

The most incredible architectural feat for Burke was the amazing Tiger Hotel, named after Burke's first mine, the Tiger-Poorman mine. The

Peace Commissioners gather for a photograph in 1890. *Left to right*: Chas. Bassett, W.H. Harris, Wyatt Earp, Luke Short, L. McLean, Bat Masterson, Neal Brown. *Courtesy of the National Archives, photo by Camillus S. Fly.*

proprietor was S.S. Glidden. It even earned its way into *Ripley's Believe It or Not!* The large hotel was composed of three stories that boasted 150 rooms, and the sole purpose was to feed and lodge the miners of the Hecla, Hercules, Tiger-Poorman and Bunker Hill mines, although locals occasionally ate at the hotel. The hotel was built right over the south fork of the Coeur d'Alene River, and the railroad tracks of the Northern Pacific and the only highway ran right "through" the middle of its first-floor lobby. The two buildings were actually connected above the river, but it did give the illusion of things running through the buildings. The hotel consisted of an older section used for boarding, which was originally built in 1888 and the second half, which was added in 1915.

Records indicate that the hotel was equipped to feed well over one thousand people daily and had to deal with five noisy passenger trains moving through the middle of the lobby every day. Unfortunately, the hotel was torn down in 1954. Not much remained of the once-flourishing town. It was reduced to a gas station, a grocery store and three saloons.

The town's elevation of 3,701 feet made it susceptible to avalanches, and several people were killed. Are any of these the spirits who many say they see peering out from the vacant windows of Burke today?

A ghost story as written in the *Rathdrum Tribune*, March 25, 1910:

Two miners working in the Hecla mine near Burke declare that the ghost of the shift boss who was killed in the recent avalanche at Mace appeared before them while they were at work in the tunnel and walked along the tunnel carrying his light and disappearing in the face of the footwall. The men were almost crazed with fear at the sight of the apparition!

The roar of the avalanche in Mace was heard by residents of Wallace five miles away. It was recorded that the slide was three thousand feet wide and buried the small town and its unfortunate residents under seventy-five feet of ice, rocks and debris. Over thirty men, women and children were buried alive and were eventually rescued, half frozen. The slide started at 11:30 p.m. on Sunday, March 1 at the top of Custer Mountain and killed at least seventy-five people.

It is possible that some of the restless spirits who roam Burke are the men who were killed during wage cuts and labor disputes in the summer of 1892. Guns were pulled when scabs (people who cross picket lines) went to work in the mines, replacing the union laborers. A stray bullet hit a box of dynamite and killed six men instantly. The fighting continued until Idaho governor Frank Steunenberg finally had enough and sent in hundreds of guardsmen to quiet the town. But the peace didn't last long.

In 1899, a group of angry miners stole a Northern Pacific Railroad train that was rolling through Burke, and as they cruised through Gem and Wallace, more men jumped aboard and joined the team. Soon, over one thousand men packed the trains with their arms full of dynamite and axes. Their target? The nearby Bunker Hill mine on McKinley Avenue in Kellogg that just fired more miners. The guardsmen from 1892 disgruntled one miner in particular, Harry Orchard (Albert Horsley). Orchard set his sights on killing the governor in retaliation, which would finally come to light later in 1905. Orchard rigged a bomb on the governor's gate at his residence in Caldwell. When the gate opened, the bomb exploded and killed Governor Steunenberg instantly. This landed Orchard a hanging sentence, which was reduced to life in prison. This was a strange sentence, as Orchard also confessed to killing up to sixteen other men in his lifetime. Orchard died at eighty-eight after spending fifty years in prison. Is it his spirit that hangs out in Burke, possibly at the abandoned Hecla mine, still wanting to support the local miners?

A major fire in 1923 also devastated the town. The *United Press Dispatch* on July 14 detailed the disaster:

Large buildings still tower over what was once the booming mining town of Burke. The vacant structures appear eerie. *Courtesy of author.*

Deep inside an abandoned mine remains the evidence of digging for silver. Many men died in the mines, as it was extremely dangerous work. *Courtesy of author.*

The town of Burke, seven miles east of here, lies in ruins as the result of a fire caused by a spark from a locomotive. Over fifty business houses of Burke's main street were destroyed and practically all of the residences are gone. Four hundred and forty miners were forced to flee to the depths of the Hecla lead and silver mine. A high wind rendered dynamite ineffectual. All of the mine company's buildings on the surface were destroyed. The damage is estimated at a million. Six hundred people are homeless. Army tents have been received from Fort George Wright at Spokane for the homeless.

The 1923 fire closed the Hecla mine temporarily and burned part of the Tiger Hotel and most of Burke to the ground. In 1933, Mr. Hanley of the Star mine bought the Tiger Hotel for $12,000. Eventually, Ed Woods bought the hotel, and it was torn down in 1954. Tourists can still view the many buildings perched among the hillsides and the gigantic Hecla mine buildings, but they are secured by chain-link fences. Littered among the debris and cool buildings are many remnants of old mining apparatus, railroad tracks, rusty metal pieces and other artifacts of another lifetime. A few residents still live in the tiny town. A small cemetery with several broken headstones is still visible. Paranormal activity is noted in the remains of Burke, and no one knows who or what haunts it.

To find the town, take exit 62 on I-90 at Wallace, Idaho, and then go north on Idaho State Highway 4. Burke is exactly seven miles up the canyon. Please *do not* disrespect the fence around the town or mines to try to explore, as it is unsafe and very dangerous. Many photographs can be found online for the curious.

GEM

Restless Miners Who Were Murdered

Gem was another small town in the Coeur d'Alene mountain area near Burke. Originally, the town was called Davenport, but the name was changed after the claim "Gem of the Mountains." During its heyday, Gem housed over two thousand people. Founded in 1886, it was nestled along Canyon Creek in the narrow area between canyons, much like Burke. Violence was popular in Gem because of many labor disputes between the miners and the mine owners. In 1892, the frustration between the union and nonunion miners met an all-time high. Guards holding Winchester rifles and miners

Left: The Frisco mine was the site of several deaths during the shootout in 1892 in the little town of Gem. *Courtesy of author.*

Below: A canary would be affected by poisonous gases before humans were, thus a signal to evacuate the mine immediately. *Courtesy of author.*

threatening to blow up buildings were everyday occurrences in Gem during these troubled times. Women and children had to be kept safe from harm and stray bullets.

Daxon's Saloon was said to be riddled with bullet holes, the owner somehow dodging them as he fled out the back door unharmed. One unarmed and unfortunate man, John Ward, was shot in his arm while standing near the White & Bender building. A nonunion man named Ivery Bean was not so lucky while he was standing between the railroad tracks and Jerry Savage's boardinghouse. He was shot, and the blame was bounced back and forth, as there were so many bullets flying through the air that it was hard to tell which one killed Bean. After the dispute settled and the miners surrendered, a total of six men were killed and sixteen were wounded. They were all taken to the nearby town of Wallace. The dead men were Ivery Bean, John Starlick, James Hennessey, Harry Cummings, August Carlson and A.T. McDonald.

The troubles did not end there. John Kneebone, an important witness for the state against the union labor trials, was working in Gem as a blacksmith, when he was harassed and threatened for weeks. The summer of 1894 would be his last. On July 3, a group of forty-plus masked and armed men surrounded Kneebone at his shop. They had come from the direction of Burke and moved in unison toward the railroad tracks by the Gem mill. When they came to Kneebone, one of the masked men said, "Well, we've got one of them," and asked the whereabouts of several other man. Soon, the workers had Doc Rogers, R.K. Neill, Foreman Crummer, Frank Higgins and Charles West. These men were able to escape and fled the area. After all was said and done, no one was arrested, as men were too scared to talk. The grand jury decided that it was not the intention of these men to kill anyone, only to scare them out of Idaho. Kneebone was just thirty-two years old. His body was buried in Wallace, Idaho, on July 6.

During Gem's more popular years, it is said that all of the trains would stop at J.H. Johnson's Saloon on their way back and forth to Burke. Once the mining was exhausted and most of the town of Burke burned down, the town of Gem slowly disappeared. Today, only a few remnants of old mining machinery can be explored as it rusts away near the river. As one looks out over the river at the scraps of metal and heavy wooden beams that can be seen from the road, it is hard to imagine such a violent scene took place at that very spot in 1892, leaving six men dead. Do the miners who were shot in cold blood still wander the dark, cold caverns inside the deep tunnels of the mines? Can their angry voices still be heard early in the morning or late at night, when the rest of the world is sleeping? Some locals claim they can see shadowy figures in the vacant buildings or hear the "tink, tink, tink" of iron on stone like some phantom is still working inside the tunnels long after they have been closed.

THE SWEETER SIDE OF GHOSTS

Not all ghost stories and hauntings have to be scary, although frightening tales are more exciting if you want to get the adrenaline going or are in need of a good scare. Many people tell stories of loved ones visiting them or premonitions received by the deceased that warn them of a danger. Others tell of full-body apparitions of friends or relatives appearing at the same moment or soon after the person has died.

Can spirits actively visit people if they wish to do so? Since countless people feel they have witnessed such events, it is possible. It is comforting to think that a loved one or best friend or even a pet can come back to visit people they shared their lives with. The spirits of animals that have passed are especially comforting, as it can be so hard when a pet passes. Included here are some stories that have been shared with me that offer the sweeter side of ghosts.

A ghost story from Rod in Wallace:

I don't really believe in ghosts, at least I didn't until I had a very strange thing happen to me. It was really early in the day and I was still trying to wake up, when I could have sworn, I saw the father of one of my best friends at the foot of my bed. I saw him clear as day. He just started at me. I stared at him. In an instant he was gone, and I figured I must have dreamed it even though I was awake. I could not shake a strange feeling all day. That evening I told my wife what had happened. She told me that he had probably died and that he was saying goodbye to me. Well, that was weird to think about. I had not talked to them in probably ten or fifteen years—not that we were not friends anymore, it's just that life gets busy and time flies by. We were very close many years ago, in fact I loved him very much and felt closer to him than my own father. I decided to check on the old man, so I made a few calls. Much to my surprise, he had passed away the very morning. I couldn't believe it. There is no other explanation than he did choose to say goodbye to me. I feel so honored and blessed to have experienced such a thing. To think a person's spirit can find a loved one in order to visit them is mind boggling. I think all he must have known about me was what state I lived in. I can't help but wonder, how did his spirit find me? How did he know where I was at the time of his death? Out of all the thousands of people he probably met in his lifetime, I feel so privileged and grateful that he chose me as one of the few people he wanted to say goodbye to. It was an experience of a lifetime. I will never forget that morning and his visit as long as I live.

A ghost story from Frannie:

I have a new house here in Idaho and there are eighteen stairs that go to the upstairs. Several times now, I have been walking up the stairs and I feel a scratching sensation on my leg. I look down, and it is actually bleeding. It really scared me to death thinking my house was possessed or a negative energy was living here with me. After about the fifth time, I couldn't take it anymore….I decided to call my girlfriend, who is psychic, and tell her about it. All I told her was, "Something strange is happening at my house."

She said, "Wait, don't tell me. Just hang on, let me think about it for a minute, OK?" I waited patiently, my nerves on edge. She finally laughed a little. I wanted to say something, but I didn't. She finally said, "It's your cat, silly!"

I said, "My cat?"

She said, "Yes, your cat you lost right before you moved. He wants you to know he is there with you, like he promised. What other way for the spirit of a cat to let you know they are there then either scratching or meowing?" I thought about it for a while. I had that cat for almost twenty years, and when I knew he was at the end of his life, I literally could not deal with it. I know he was holding on just for me when he was so tired and weak. The night he died I had a long "talk" with him and told him it was OK for him to go and that we would always be together and that I loved him so very much. We had been through two decades of life events together, and he was always there for me no matter what. I told him to come back and be with me if he could. He died in my arms. I was devastated. I did not know I could love an animal that much. I physically felt pain in my chest at losing him. The following week I was sleeping, and I could have sworn I felt a cat jumping up on the bed and settle in by my legs like he always did. It happened several times. It made me feel very happy. I knew it was the spirit of my beloved cat. After I moved from that house where he is buried I did not have any more experiences like that, which kinda made me sad. So, I was thrilled when she told me it was my loving cat still with me.

His feline ghost had followed me and is here with me. That night I had a little "talk" with him, saying I knew he was there and that it made me very happy to have him with me but that I could do without the scratches. I have never had another episode of being scratched since. It does bring my heart good knowing that our treasured pets have spirits and can continue to love us even in the afterlife. I don't really care if people think I am crazy. I know what happened and I know the deep love me and that cat shared.

A ghost story from Sue:

I always smell cigarettes and perfume when I miss my mother. There are no cigarettes or that perfume in my house. She smoked a lot and wore a very particular fragrance. I love the fact that she can somehow do this from wherever she is at because I miss her so much. It is very comforting to think that our loved ones can contact us in strange ways but in ways we know it can only be them.

A ghost story told by Victoria in Mullan, Idaho:

His piercing blue eyes seemed to look right through you, and at first, they took me back. But as I got to know him, I found they were windows to the incredible heart inside. This aging sixty-five-year-old had more depth inside of him than those blue eyes could ever convey to a stranger but became expressive and kind as I knew him more. Incredibly kind, loving, patriotic and respectful, we developed a quick friendship that I treasured with my entire being. As our friendship progressed, I began to look to him for advice, knowledge and philosophy. He was a world of information and opinion that was something I drew upon regularly. His tall, thin frame would make you think that he was somehow frail. But he was a strong man who could accomplish anything. I could recognize him anywhere, as that thin frame was offset by a set of large ears that protruded from his head. A bit funny really, but they were simply part of what made him different from everyone else in a crowd. But there was a sad part of him that I always wished I could fix. He'd lost his wife of forty years just five years previous. In his home, he kept everything exactly as she had left it on the day of her death. He wanted nothing moved, no one to go into her bedroom or disturb any element of her past presence in their home. She was his ghost that he longed to see just one last time if he could.

He'd conveyed to me how he wished that he would have been sweeter to her during their marriage. He told me that he hadn't known such appreciation for her and everything she had brought to his life until she became ill with cancer. Suddenly, she was the most important thing to him, and regret filled his heart as he watched her die. Carl Lass and I became very close friends over the years and regularly dined out for our fabulous conversations. November 2 of 1980, he had a dinner date planned. When we always called to confirm a few hours before, this time I didn't hear from him.

I called his house numerous times with no answer, so I left message after message. I made excuses. He forgot, he went to see his relatives in another city, he made other plans and blew me off. I let it go. That night, I didn't sleep well at all. I began to worry. By 10:00 a.m., I felt a sense of panic and urgency, got into my car and drove over to his house. He'd given me a key to his garage, so I used it to let myself in. His car was there, and the panic worsened. As I headed up the stairs to the main living area, I opened the door, looked into the living room and saw him slumped in his recliner, eyes open and staring right at me. I expected him to blink, to become startled at my entry from the stairway. But he didn't. He just continued to stare, and I realized he might be ill in some way and needing help. I screamed his name, threw my keys down and ran to him.

That first touch was completely devastating, as his body was ice cold. I knew he was dead, and my heart was broken. Suddenly, there was a fear inside of me that came to the surface in the form of tears streaming down my face. I'd lost him. I'd lost him, and it was all my fault. In my mind, if I would have been more concerned the night before, I could have come over and maybe saved him if he were having a health event of some sort. I ran to call 911. "I just found my friend dead!" I screamed into the phone as I cried hysterically. The operator asked for his address, but I didn't know it by heart. She was becoming very frustrated with me and yelled to go outside and look at the numbers on the house. Phone in hand, I did just that as I shook and couldn't stop shaking and crying.

The policeman who showed up was so kind and sat with me as his family members arrived and the mortuary came to remove his body. I watched as the family members didn't even go to him. Instead, they immediately began loading their cars with his precious belongings, going through every drawer, cupboard and closet. They went into his wife's sacred room and removed her jewelry and trinkets. It was sickening and sad. I asked the policeman if he could stop them and he said, "No, I don't have that authority." I went to his funeral but refused to go to the wake with his disgusting family. I just couldn't pretend to have respect for them at all. I instead went home to lay on the sofa, where I fell asleep and dreamed of finding him again. When I awoke with a sudden jerk, my little poodle was lying on my chest, her head under my chin, and I knew she was trying to comfort me in some way. I hugged her intensely and cried like a baby.

I found out later that he had died of a heart attack. I always wondered if it had actually been a broken heart. But remembering back to the look on his face, it wasn't one of trauma or shock. The look on his face was as if it had been simply frozen in time. His death had been instant, I was told. As time passed after his death, dreams of finding him haunted me more. Over and over, I had the same dream. I had them regularly, as if I were reliving the entire day to have a different outcome.

Within two years, I started seeing his blue Buick sedan—him driving it—in my rearview mirror as I would be driving somewhere. But as soon as I turned around, it would turn out to be a school bus, a Volkswagen bug or maybe a pickup truck. My heart would sink, and I would again become so sad. I lived with the guilt daily. A sickening, sad feeling. A wish that I could go back and change what I did or didn't do. One night, as I lay in my bed in a large bedroom at the base of the stairs, I was just drifting off to sleep when I heard my poodle begin to growl. The growl seemed odd and seemed to come from deep in her little throat. This deep growl alerted me to the fact that she was seeing something on my side of the bed. As I turned my head to face my side of the bed, I realized that my hand was up in the air and being held by a man—a tall, thin figure with large ears. I wasn't instantly frightened, since the hands holding mine so gently were warm and soothing.

This figure of a man began to lean down toward me, his face nearly visible in the light from the staircase. I was anxious to see who this figure was, and as the light slowly spread across his face, my poodle suddenly bust into a frantic bark, jumped off the bed and darted up the stairs. Suddenly, I felt frightened. She would never bark at nothing. I was shocked into complete conscience now, and I scrambled out of bed and ran up the stairs after her. She knew something I didn't. At the top stair, a realization came over me, and I turned tail and scampered back down the stairs. At the bottom, there in the dim light, I saw he was gone. I called his name, "Carl, Carl! Come back!" I knew it was him, and I felt sorry that I hadn't stayed for the complete experience. I sat on the bed and cried for a few moments. No longer scared, I knew why he was there. I dwelled on it for days, not telling anyone of my ghostly event. Strangely, I never had the dream again, I never again saw him in my rearview mirror, and I never again felt the guilt that had plagued me since his death.

Somehow, I knew he had come back to tell me, "Just stop. It wasn't your fault." He never came to me again, but I always wished he would. Just so that I, like he with his wife, could see him one last time.

CONCLUSION

Stories of ghosts, hauntings and restless spirits have been around as long as living people have been alive, and they will continue until the end of time. Perhaps people are fascinated by them because they want some sort of proof that there is life after death; they desire to know their loved ones are not suffering or they simply think ghostly tales are interesting.

As technology advances, the desire to capture proof of spirits' existence has increased dramatically and is no longer limited to Ouija boards, crystal balls, tea leaves, psychics and slate writers. People do not frown on those who choose to believe in ghosts and the spirit world as much as they did in the past. It is common to hear conversations about ghosts and spirits almost everywhere you go. Many paranormal groups are popping up all over the place, their members eager to prove the existence of ghosts.

As for Coeur d'Alene, it has tugged at people's hearts since early development with its charm, beauty and the serenity of the nearby water. The Silver Valley continues to bless its citizens with treasures from deep in the mountains, offering silver, ore and gold to those willing to search for it.

I am hoping my mixture of local history and hauntings in my books continue to enrich readers' lives and encourage others to explore the various places revealed. I have many teachers and parents thank me for my books and tell me that they cannot get their students and children to read or get interested in history but that my books have opened the door for both of these things. For that, I am very proud and happy.

The historic Feehan House in Murray is a rare example of a home that was built of logs and not dimensional wood. *Courtesy of author.*

And as locals and tourists roam in and out of the local stores or enjoy a libation in an old hotel or bar, I hope that they find these stories from the past fascinating, frightening and intriguing. I also hope this book makes them stop in the entryways of the Roosevelt Inn and the Ryan Hotel or as they walk through old forts and cemeteries. I hope they pause for just a second or two to remember those early pioneers, who worked so hard to create the wonderful towns that everyone loves today.

And who knows, maybe they will even spot a dark apparition lurking in a corner somewhere or hear the faint whispers of a restless ghost asking for help. Hopefully, they might feel the lightest touch of a cold hand as a ghost tries to caress the side of their face as they slowly turn to walk away.

Happy hauntings!

BIBLIOGRAPHY

Coeur d'Alene Press. "Hotel Man Disappears." December 13, 1906.
————. "They Dug Up Bones." June 1, 1901.
Derig, Betty. *Roadside History of Idaho*. Missoula, MT: Mountain Press Publishing, 1996.
"Descriptions of Occupations: Mines and Mining." United States Bureau of Labor Statistics. Cornell University Library. Ithaca, New York, 1918.
Dolph, Jerry, and Arthur Randall. *Wyatt Earp and the Coeur d'Alene Gold!* Coeur d'Alene: Museum of North Idaho, 1999.
Entze, Marc, comp. "Mullan Road Workforce and Supplies Required to Complete the Mullan Road John Mullan to A.A. Humphreys." October 25, 1869.
Evening Capital News. "Both Sides Rest in the Rossi Trial." October 13, 1916.
The Great 1910 Fire. "Fatalities." http://1910fire.com.
"The Hahn Mansion." *Ghost Writer* (blog). https://spiritedwriter.wordpress.com.
Helena Independent. "The Gem Murder." July 13, 1894.
Hobson, George C. *Gems of Thought & the History of Shoshone County*. Kellogg, IK: Kellogg Evening News Press, 1940.
Kalispell Bee. "Bones Tell the Story." December 22, 1903.
Kendrick Gazette. "Idaho Cities Buried under Avalanche." March 11, 1910.
"L.L. Sweet." In *Illustrated History of North Idaho*, 1,067. Spokane, WA: Western Historical Publishing, 1903.
Lewiston Inter-State News. "How Towns Were Named." April 21, 1905.

"1972 Sunshine Mining Company Mining Disaster." *Mine Disasters* (blog). August 22, 2007. https://minedisasters.blogspot.com.

Silver City Nugget. "A $1,000,000 jackass." March 27, 1903.

Silver Messenger. "Skeletons Found." December 29, 1903.

Spokane Daily Chronicle. "Rossi Is Not Guilty of Murder." October 14, 1916.

"Theodore F. Jameson." In *Illustrated History of North Idaho*, 1,202. Spokane, WA: Western Historical Publishing, 1903.

Twin Falls Times. "Hunts for Lost Treasure." December 9, 1913.

Weiser, Kathy. "Patsy Clark, Mining Magnate & the Haunted Clark Mansion." Legends of America. Updated December 2010. https://www.legendsofamerica.com.

Wood River Times. "Peace and War." July 20, 1892. Reprinted from *Wallace Free Press.* July 16, 1892.

ABOUT THE AUTHOR

Originally from upstate New York, Deborah Cuyle loves everything about small towns. She has also written *Kidding Around Portland, Oregon*; *Cannon Beach, Oregon*; *Haunted Snohomish*; *Ghosts of Leavenworth and the Cascade Foothills*; and *Haunted Everett*. Her passions include local history, animals, museums, hiking and horseback riding. Deborah enjoys thinking about the possibility of an afterlife and especially loves telling a chilling ghost story while nestled beside a bonfire with her best friends and family. She and her husband are currently remodeling a haunted house in Wallace, Idaho.

www.ingramcontent.com/pod-product-compliance
Lightning Source LLC
Chambersburg PA
CBHW040409110426
42812CB00012B/2500